A Director's Guide

Management buy-outs

THE CRITICAL SUCCESS FACTORS
FOR DIRECTORS

D1437890

h

...or. Lesley Shutte

Production Manager: Victoria Davies
Production Editor: Alex Grant
Head of Business Development: Simon Seward
Design: Halo Design
Chairman: Tim Melville-Ross
Managing Director: Andrew Main Wilson

Published for the Institute of Directors and Phildrew Ventures
by Director Publications Ltd
116 Pall Mall London SW1Y 5ED

Editorial: 0171 766 8910
Sponsorship: 0171 766 8885
Production: 0171 766 8960
Facsimile: 0171 766 8990

YOURS TO HAVE AND TO HOLD
BUT NOT TO COPY

Director Publications Ltd
116 Pall Mall
London SW1Y 5ED

Kogan Page Ltd
120 Pentonville Road
London N1 9JN

© Director Publications 1998

British Library Cataloguing in Publication Data
A CIP record for this book is available from the British Library
ISBN 0 7494 2828 7

Printed and bound in Great Britain by St Ives plc

Contents

— — — — — — —

— — — — — — —

— — — — — — —

— — — — — — —●

WHEN YOU'RE C.E.O. YOU CAN WRITE YOUR OWN HEADLINES.

How do you like your headlines? Short? Or slightly more on the long side? Do you want them in glorious Technicolour? Or just black and white? The point is when you're the boss you decide. And if you like the idea of making decisions you might want to consider an **MBO** or **MBI**.

That's where we come in as advisors to funds of over £410 million we have expertise to put you in command. And since we've already completed over 80 such transactions of £10 million or more, our team has the experience to act quickly on your behalf. Start calling the shots. Just call us on **0171 628 6366**.

PHILDREW ◆ VENTURES

Creative Capital for Management Buy-Outs

PHILDREW VENTURES, TRITON COURT, 14 FINSBURY SQUARE, LONDON EC2A 1PD. TEL 0171 628 6366

PHILDREW VENTURES IS REGULATED BY IMRO AND IS AN ASSOCIATE OF UBS ASSET MANAGEMENT LONDON LTD.

Directors and buy-out opportunities

Tim Melville-Ross, Director General, Institute of Directors

In recent years, management buy-outs and buy-ins have been an important facet in the creation of a more enterprise-friendly culture in the UK, with successful deals releasing the wealth-creating talents and energies of many British directors and managers.

At present, buy-outs are benefiting from a relatively benign economic climate and a wide availability of venture capital backing for the right deals. Even so, the MBO is not a process to be undertaken lightly. Companies in the nineties carry the burden of many legal obligations – and an MBO adds to these. The stress of the deal on the director in a personal capacity, plus extra strains on the company and its employees, should not be underestimated. It is a lengthy process, involving many days of negotiations and close scrutiny of legal and financial documents. At the same time, the company must continue to function as normally as possible.

Nevertheless, to go through a management buy-out and emerge successful is one of the most exciting and fulfilling achievements a director can accomplish. An MBO is demanding and it can be fraught with risk. But it is a process that proves the commitment of a management team to its company and it enhances directors' understanding of their business and its future potential. In these respects it is an important learning process for many business men and women.

Careful planning, commitment, hard work and sound advice are the main factors in a successful MBO. This guide, written by leading experts, contains clear, practical advice on the key aspects of MBOs from the first thoughts of a deal through to the elation of a triumphant "exit". It will prove an indispensable aid to any director contemplating participating in a buy-out.

AUTUMN? IT'S SPRING TIME

Are you ready to fade into the mists of obscurity? Accept the decline towards the winter of your days? Or is this the time for a new company to bloom? With you in charge, naturally. Consider an MBO or MBI and let us help you flourish. As advisors to funds of over £410 million we have the expertise to make budding ideas a reality. And since we've already completed over 80 such transactions of £10 million or more, our experienced team is ready to act swiftly on your behalf. Start sowing the seeds now and call us on **0171 628 6366**.

PHILDREW VENTURES

Creative Capital for Management Buy-Outs

PHILDREW VENTURES, TRITON COURT, 14 FINSBURY SQUARE, LONDON EC2A 1PD. TEL 0171 628 6366

PHILDREW VENTURES IS REGULATED BY IMRO AND IS AN ASSOCIATE OF UBS ASSET MANAGEMENT LONDON LTD.

A steady flow of fresh prospects

Katharine Campbell, Growing Business Correspondent, Financial Times

The buy-out market has been humming. Would-be entrepreneurs have been fed a steady supply of fresh prospects as large public companies restructure and dispose of non-core assets. Again, the lifecycle of the family business – posing the perennial question of succession – repeatedly throws up favourable conditions for an MBO or MBI attempt.

In 1996, the volume of UK buy-outs and buy-ins increased 43 per cent to £7.8bn, exceeding the previous record set in 1989, according to the Centre for Management Buy-Out Research at Nottingham University. 1997 was another very busy year in the UK – and in continental Europe too, where there is a growing awareness of the merits of the buy-out as a means of revivifying neglected businesses and generally unleashing entrepreneurial energy.

Private equity managers have enjoyed handsome returns from deals cut during the recession of the early nineties that have been exited via a stockmarket flotation or a sale to a trade buyer in the recent clement environment. Consequently, they are raising ever bigger investment funds with ease – and pressure to spend the new money is considerable.

But ample supplies of equity – and debt – are not unadulterated good news for the aspiring buy-out manager. Keen competition between institutions has led to some heady prices being paid for businesses at the moment. That in turn can mean that managers are offered a significantly smaller stake in the buy-out than was the case a few years ago.

And there is the danger of economic slowdown – even recession – always lurking. So it pays more than ever to have your wits about you in today's fast-changing market. The following authoritative chapters will help you get to grips with the considerable complexities of a buy-out or buy-in, and guide you through what should ultimately be a very rewarding – if demanding – experience. Good luck.

THE VENTURER OF THE YEAR AWARD 1997

OVERALL WINNER

Presented to

Ultra Electronics Holdings plc

Venture capital provider

Phildrew Ventures

JUDGING PANEL

MR DEREK BONHAM	THE ENERGY GROUP	MR DAVID QUYSNER	ABINGWORTH MANAGEMENT LTD
MR ALAN BOWKETT	BERISFORD PLC	MR GRAEME ROBINSON	ERNST & YOUNG
MR RONALD HAMILTON	INTERFACE VENTURES	MR ALASTAIR ROSS GOOBEY	HERMES PENSION FUND MANAGERS
MR RICHARD LAMBERT	THE FINANCIAL TIMES	MR CLIVE SHERLING	APAX PARTNERS & CO VENTURES LTD
MR JOHN LEIGHFIELD	RESEARCH MACHINES PLC	MR ROBERT SMITH	MORGAN GRENFELL ASSET
	BIRMINGHAM MIDSHIRES BUILDING		MANAGEMENT LTD
	SOCIETY	SIR RICHARD SYKES	GLAXO WELLCOME PLC
MR GEORGE MAGAN	NATWEST MARKETS CORPORATE	SIR ANTHONY TENNANT	MORGAN STANLEY & CO LTD
	ADVISORY LTD	SIR MARTIN WOOD OBE	OXFORD INSTRUMENTS PLC
DR KEITH MCCULLAGH	BRITISH BIOTECH PLC	MR ROBERT WORCESTER	MORI LTD
MR NORMAN MURRAY	MORGAN GRENFELL DEVELOPMENT	THE RT HON LORD YOUNG	YOUNG ASSOCIATES LTD
	CAPITAL	OF GRAFFHAM PC	

Sponsored by

FINANCIAL TIMES   *Cartier*   BVCA

Chapter 1

MBO stars

Philip Beresford, business writer and author of the Sunday Times' Rich List survey, looks at the personalities behind some of the UK's most successful buy-outs

The National Lottery has just one serious rival in the matter of millionaire creation – namely the management buy-out. In the last four years alone, more than 255 millionaire directors have been created by management buy-outs and buy-ins, according to *Director* magazine's own annual performance guide to the MBO sector. But while the lottery route to wealth simply requires enormous luck and the spending of £1 on those six numbers, the MBO/MBI involves risk-taking, sheer hard work and some well-honed management skills. So who are some of the stars in the MBO firmament – the risk-takers who have often succeeded against all the odds?

POLICEMAN TURNED BUSINESSMAN

Derek Hunt, the former policeman, who chairs the MFI Furniture Group, is the biggest risk taker of them all. He led the £715m buy-out of the business in the heady days of October 1987. It was the biggest leveraged buy-out in British history at the time. But what timing. Within two weeks, Black Monday hammered the stockmarket. Hunt later admitted that he was absolutely terrified that the staff and managers who had sunk savings and mortgaged their homes would lose the lot. The recession of the early nineties did not help, but Hunt and his management team stuck with it when many rivals foundered.

What did help was the strong reputation Hunt and his managers had in the City. Furthermore, MFI was able to exploit both the benefits of vertical integration and its early investment in electronic point of sales. In 1992, MFI had made sufficient progress to float on the stockmarket, netting Hunt a bonus of £1.3m. He retains shares and options which are together worth at least the same again.

Unlike the lottery millionaires – who quite literally make it in an instant – Hunt and his managers had to graft for years. At the float, each of MFI's executive directors had been with the business for at least 13 years. Hunt himself joined in 1972. Twenty-five years later he is still going as strong as ever.

Other buy-outs result from some very nifty footwork by executives in large businesses. Gerry Robinson was a trouble-shooter for GrandMet dispatched to turn ailing subsidiaries round. In two years, he turned an £11m loss in its contract services division into a £10m profit. GrandMet decided to sell, and it was at this point that Robinson's hour came. As Lord Sheppard, chairman at the time, later recalled: "Gerry asked me if I would give him 48 hours to put together an offer. I said: "You've got 24 hours," and, 24 hours later, he was back with bankers and a formal approach." A £160m buy-out was agreed and a year later, in 1988, the business – now called Compass – was floated, netting Robinson a £12m fortune. But the experience merely whetted Robinson's appetite for bigger challenges. In 1991, he moved to Granada and built it up to be one of the UK's major businesses following bitter takeover battles for London Weekend Television, and more famously, the Forte hotel and catering empire.

MINE'S A DOUBLE

Similarly, Sir Paul Judge, the high-flying Cadbury Schweppes planning director, was asked to arrange the sale of its food and drinks operation in 1986. Offers from would-be purchasers came in way below the asset value of the business. But Judge reckoned the business could be turned around, so justifying a higher offer. "I went to Dominic (Cadbury) to ask if I could put in a bid," he said. Within a week, Judge had £80m of venture capital backing and the £97m buy-out of what was to become Premier Brands was completed. Judge hoped to float the business, but in the event, the board accepted a £195m offer from Hillsdown Holdings within three years of the buy-out.

Judge left the company over the sale which made the directors and many of the employees very wealthy. Under the terms of the deal, the Premier shares held by the staff had multiplied in value by 500 times as the business performance improved sharply and debt was pared right back. Judge departed with £45m. The other directors held stakes averaging £15m each. However, rather than retiring to spend his wealth, Judge went to work in politics and the venture capital industry. He also gave £8m of his fortune to help fund a management school at Cambridge – appropriately called the Judge Institute of Management Studies. Judge was an early proponent of worker capitalism, with Premier's workers able to buy 1,000 share options for £20. At the sale, those same options were worth £5,000 – an extraordinary demonstration of the power of the buy-out.

EVERYONE'S A WINNER

Premier was not alone in extending the buy-out from management to staff as a whole. There were two classic examples in the eighties. In 1987, the Unipart motor components group was bought out by management and staff from Rover. Under chief executive John Neil, the group has been transformed and has pioneered a huge investment programme in training and educating its 3,500 staff. They own 46 per cent of the shares, which have appreciated by 46,000 per cent since the buy-out. The average holding of 4,100 shares held by the staff is currently worth £9,340 and there are several millionaires in the management led by Neil, whose six million shares are worth £12m.

Unipart has not yet floated and its shares are valued on an internal market. But that other pioneer of worker capitalism, NFC Holdings – formerly the National Freight Consortium – was an employee buy-out from the government in 1982 for what proved a snip at £53m. Sir Peter Thompson, who led the buy-out and the later float in 1989, has been described as the 'grandfather' of the MBO for his pioneering work in the field. It has been lucrative too. He made several million pounds from the float. Now retired from the business, Sir Peter is still involved in several other ventures. NFC has had some problems in the nineties, but after some sweeping management changes appears to be back on track as a leading logistics group.

A POSITIVE EXPLOSION

The nineties has seen a positive explosion of MBO activity. Figures compiled by KPMG Corporate Finance show that in 1996, the total funding for bigger MBOs (of over £10m each) reached £5.91bn, just pipping the previous record in 1989.

As FT "blue-chips" have become leaner and more focused in their business activities, so businesses perceived as peripheral have been sold by the score to their existing managers or a new management team. Hand-in-hand with this development, venture capital has truly come of age in the UK. As Frank Neale, a partner at Phildrew Ventures puts it, when comparing the eighties to today: "There are more venture capitalists fighting and killing each other for the deal than there were last time."

As a result, a whole host of new MBO stars have emerged. Michael Peagram, chairman of Holliday Chemicals, was a successful salaried executive who was given the chance to turn round what was then an ailing chemicals business. He spent £50,000 of his own money on a 24 per cent stake in the business in 1985.

Within weeks of joining he reckoned he had probably lost all his money as the position was grim. But he pulled the company round, and led a buy-out in 1987. Six years later, a revamped Holliday was floated. Peagram's initial £50,000 is now worth £26m, but it has not made much difference to his life: asked the ritual question about when he is going to buy a yacht, his answer is always a snort of laughter.

At BTG – formerly British Technology Group – many of the staff could be forgiven for thinking about yachts and the like. With a heap of licences for exciting inventions in its stable, BTG was bought by staff and management in 1992 for £27.5m from the government. In 1995, it floated on the stockmarket with a price tag of £39.4m. Since then the shares have soared as the City enthused about BTG's portfolio; in June 1997, BTG was capitalised at over £590m. Ian Harvey, BTG's chief executive, is currently sitting on a £4.5m share stake, while options awarded to the staff at the float are now worth an average of two years' salary.

PROFITS FROM PAINKILLERS

Perhaps the most unusual MBO in terms of product has been Meconic, the Edinburgh-based pharmaceuticals company which was bought from Glaxo by its management in 1990. For Meconic is the UK's only legal supplier of opiates for pain relief and other medical applications. Around 70 managers and staff held 40 per cent of the shares in the £17.4m buy-out. Five years later, the business was floated with a £44.4m valuation. Strong growth had lifted its stockmarket value to £125m by mid-1997. Three of the four executive directors were also paper millionaires led by Dr Henry Smalley, managing director, with a near £6m stake.

The appetite for buy-outs looks set to last and their role in millionaire creation will no doubt rival the National Lottery in the foreseeable future. Indeed, the scope for new millionaire-creating sectors seems endless. A whole raft of wealth has emerged from the newly-privatised rail sector. Who would take bets against an MBO from whatever form of private sector involvement is chosen for the currently cash-strapped London Underground? Bakerloo PLC or Piccadilly Holdings could throw up some new stars for future surveys.

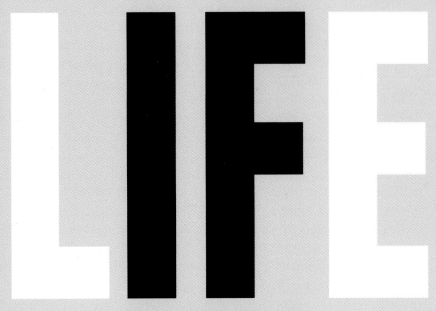

LIFE

LIFE IS FULL OF IFS.

What if? What if you go for that MBO or MBI of £10 million or more? And what if it comes off? At Phildrew Ventures we're here to help you with all these ifs. As advisors to funds of over £400 million, we can offer a friendly and approachable team who are with you every step of the way.

And if it's experience you're after, we've already completed over 60 such transactions. You'll also be dealing with our most senior people who can act decisively on your behalf. So no more ifs. Give us a call today on 0171 628 6366 and we'll get on the case straight away.

PHILDREW ❖ VENTURES

Creative Capital for Management Buy-Outs

PHILDREW VENTURES, TRITON COURT, 14 FINSBURY SQUARE, LONDON EC2A 1PD. TEL 0171 628 6366

PHILDREW VENTURES IS REGULATED BY IMRO AND IS AN ASSOCIATE OF UBS ASSET MANAGEMENT LONDON LTD.

Chapter 2

Buy-outs: boom or bust?

Professor Ken Robbie and Professor Mike Wright of Nottingham University's Centre for Management Buy-Out Research, (CMBOR), assess the UK's recent buy-out scene and highlight the increasing popularity of hybrid deals

Buy-outs in the UK and continental Europe reached record values in 1997 with the number of transactions recorded in the UK also achieving a new peak. However, there are concerns that these boom conditions may be followed by a period of serious retrenchment if too many deals are funded at excessive prices and with financing structures which cannot be serviced from cashflow.

During 1997, the total value of UK buy-outs and buy-ins increased by 35 per cent to £10.5bn. This level of activity meant a record high for the second year in succession. While the rising size of deal was a major factor behind the increase in the total value of transactions (the average value increased from £12.2m to £15.2m), the total volume also increased to a record 694. The growth in numbers over the past three years has been associated with a significant increase in buy-outs from private owners (including secondary buy-outs from venture capital firms) and until the General Election public sector privatisation. Trends into 1998 continued the buoyancy of 1997. In the first half of 1998, a total of £8bn worth of deals were completed, although their number was down on the same period of 1997.

The high level of activity has also increased the relative importance of buy-outs and buy-ins in the overall UK takeover market. Once again 1997 saw them accounting for over half the number of such transactions, with a record share of 59 per cent being achieved, highlighting the acceptance of buy-outs as a permanent feature of corporate restructuring in the UK.

The pattern of recent growth has not been uniform across the buy-out market. A major feature has been the re-emergence of externally initiated transactions. Although traditionally these have been management buy-ins, the past three years or so have seen the rapid development of two other forms – the hybrid management buy-in/buy-out (BIMBO) and the investor buy-out (IBO). Buy-ins (including BIMBOs and IBOs) strengthened their position in terms of deal value in the first half of 1998, at £5.6bn accounting for a record 71 per cent of the market. This amount of funds invested was the highest half-year value of buy-ins ever recorded.

The development of the BIMBO was a response to the generally poor record of buy-ins in the late eighties. With receivership rates of about a third for deals completed in this period a major re-assessment of buy-ins was necessary. Some of the problems resulted from an all too easy ability to overpay for acquisitions and relatively high gearing in the late eighties, which could not withstand the subsequent recessionary period. An extremely important factor was also the failure of venture capitalists and new management to correctly identify problem areas during due diligence. Completing a deal jointly with selected internal management could be expected to significantly reduce such risks.

THE IBO MARKET

Development of the IBO market has been spectacular over the past three years, with £3.5bn worth of transactions being recorded by Nottingham University's Centre for Management Buy-Out Research (CMBOR) in 1997. The number of IBOs rose from 29 to 50. The trend has continued into 1998: in the first quarter of the year, seven out of the nine deals with a transaction value over £100m were IBOs.

In a typical IBO, a venture capital firm will have been asked to engage in an auction for a large divestment transaction. This process may be conducted directly by the vendor but more frequently through an intermediary. The venture capital firm may not have direct access to management until they become a shortlisted bidder or even later. Consequently the venture capital firm may have to consider head-hunting a new CEO or indeed managing the company itself.

While larger companies will tend to have much more developed accounting and financial systems than many smaller buy-ins, significant problems can still emerge in due diligence, especially given the time constraints of analysing businesses which are frequently international in operating structure. Additionally, auction inspired competition may result in over-paying for a business.

The development of the IBO reflects both vendor and venture capital firm considerations. For the vendor, increasing emphasis on shareholder value at a time of relative economic buoyancy has encouraged the development of auctions. Major divestors are well aware of the interest of venture capital firms in acquiring companies. Additionally, vendors may be concerned that in larger divestments, sales proceeds may not be maximised if management are closely involved at an early stage, especially if they are also considering their own buy-out transaction.

In recent years, venture capital firms have been extremely successful in raising funds. However, they are faced with the prospect of having to invest these large sums prudently, while also being seen to be completing deals. Such factors have led not only to a willingness to compete in auctions but also to a much more proactive approach in identifying potential transactions ahead of rivals.

SECONDARY BUY-OUTS

A further major development in recent years has concerned exit routes, with 1996 being a record year for realisations of investments in buy-outs and buy-ins. Receiverships have been low in line with general economic and financial conditions, while the number of trade sales has risen rapidly. However, in 1997 the total number of buy-out and buy-in exits fell. Flotations were particularly badly affected, down from 40 to 28, with this trend continuing into 1998.

The increase in secondary buy-outs has been a particularly notable development in exits, while at the same time creating new deals. In these transactions, the original buy-out is refinanced with a new ownership structure, sometimes involving the original venture capital backer exiting and or a second-tier management team or external management team taking over. In excess of 200 such deals have now been completed.

Although 1996 was a record year with 39 secondary buy-outs and buy-ins identified, 1997 saw some easing back in deal numbers to 32. These secondary buy-outs may be triggered by a number of factors. Management may resist alternative exit plans put forward by the venture capital firm because of a long-term desire to remain independent. There may, however, be a need for additional funding for the company to allow a major expansion which cannot otherwise be met if the company is to remain independent and private. In such cases, venture capital firms may be pressing for their own exit where they are constrained by limited-life equity funds.

SERIAL ENTREPRENEURS

An interesting related area has been the emergence of serial entrepreneurs in the UK. These are entrepreneurs who have been backed by venture capitalists in an initial buy-out or buy-in from which they have exited, and who now want to be financed again in another venture. This development has not only given the venture capital industry a source of entrepreneurial management with an established track record (making management evaluation theoretically easier) but has helped to generate deals through the supply of propositions from people who understand how the venture capital industry works.

The past few years have seen a major increase in entry prices for buy-outs and buy-ins. This has been particularly marked for the larger transactions where competition tends to be greater. The last complete year of buy-out activity, 1997, saw a marked increase in the entry prices for deals with a value over £25m. The average entry PE ratio, measured by the ratio of transaction value to historic earnings before interest, increased in 1997 from 12.2 to 13.3. This rise was mainly accounted for by increases in entry prices for buy-in type transactions. Entry PE ratios for larger IBOs increased in 1996 to 12.8, but eased back in 1997 to 11.8.

Financial structuring has been affected by the considerable liquidity of most fund suppliers as well as competition between players to win transaction mandates. The proportion of equity in buy-out and buy-in deal structures has been falling steadily since 1992.

Although the senior debt element in deals has not risen to the levels seen in the late eighties, other forms of quasi-debt have become more important. Relaxations in interest coverage ratios may encourage more marginal deals. The proportion of larger buy-outs – particularly those funded by mezzanine, loan notes and other forms of financing – has risen considerably. The total amount of mezzanine in larger buy-outs rose to £592m in 1997 – its second highest level – although still well behind the record year of 1989.

JUNK BONDS

An important new development in the UK has been the adoption of high-yield bond instruments, so-called "junk bonds", which have been used in some new buy-outs and for a further significant innovation in the market, the leveraged build-up. These involve the development of a group of companies based on an initial buy-out to which major acquisitions are added. For private equity backers, these may offer a means of achieving the higher returns required to offset increasing entry prices.

Associated with the development of junk bonds has been the recent growth of an "alphabet loan market" for large UK buy-outs. Where there is a need to restructure the business it may be preferable to delay capital repayments, so as to retain cashflow inside the company, then instruments may be used which have either a one- or two-year repayment holiday and/or instruments that are only repayable in one payment when the company is sold or floated at a pre-determined date.

Where it is economically viable for debt providers to separate these instruments, more than one layer of senior debt may be provided. In these cases, the "A" loan typically has a seven-year life, while "B" and, if applicable, "C" loans generally have longer maturity and nominal amortisation prior to repayment of the "A" loan, with higher rates of interest to compensate. These debt layers have equal priority in the event of default. Buy-outs from private vendors rose to record levels in 1996, exceeding those from UK divestors for the first time. This trend continued into 1997, with 45 per cent of buy-outs from this source. High selling prices combined with concerns over potential changes in tax are likely to have been factors behind this growth in buy-outs of family-owned businesses.

A notable feature of recent developments is the re-emergence of buy-out type deals involving companies quoted on a stockmarket which subsequently de-list (known as "going privates"). This kind of deal came to prominence in the UK during the eighties market boom, peaking at almost a third of market value in 1989. These buy-outs subsequently fell away during the recession of the early nineties, but have recently recovered.

FUTURE OUTLOOK

The picture which is now emerging is one of a highly liquid industry where venture capital firms are competing keenly for new transactions. In such circumstances the market could over-heat (as in the late eighties). Although 1997 was a record year for nominal deal value, in real terms it was only 65 per cent of the 1989 peak. However, the sharp rise in activity in the first half of 1998 and increases in debt levels and entry PE ratios, take the market closer to these levels.

The main economic and financial indicators have provided a background for the buy-out industry to develop over the last three to four years which is more stable than that of the late eighties. This may be coming to an end given concerns about the impact of international factors on the UK economy and the possibility of recession looming ahead. At present it does not seem that the market is heading for the kind of meltdown seen at the end of the eighties, but short-term prospects are beginning to look more uncertain, producing a need for caution especially among the larger valued and more highly priced transactions. Over the last 15 years the buy-out market has shown itself to be remarkably adaptable whatever the nature of economic conditions. Despite the uncertainties it seems likely that the market will see a continued strong supply of buy-outs of solid small to medium-sized businesses.

Chapter 3

Choosing a venture capital partner

Frank Neale, partner at Phildrew Ventures, says that for a deal to succeed the emphasis should be on partnership

Before you set out to find a venture capital partner, it is vital to understand the true nature of venture capital. Venture capital is all about a business partnership based on equity investment. In a management buy-out transaction the venture capitalist takes on numerous roles, in particular:

- *Identifying potential opportunities;*

- *Evaluating targets to ensure an MBO would work;*

- *Negotiating the deal with the vendor;*

- *Arranging the finance;*

- *Undertaking due diligence;*

- *Managing the whole process to ensure a deal takes place;*

- *Post-investment support and monitoring;*

- *Handling the approach to the exit.*

KEY CRITERIA

Before you actually make the decision on a particular venture capitalist, it is helpful if you set down the criteria upon which you are going to base your judgement. When you are researching venture capitalists and meeting them, you can develop your questioning around these criteria. The factors you should consider include:

- *Financial objectives;*

- *Size of transaction;*

- *Funds available;*

- *Type of deal;*

- *Sector experience;*

- *Geographic location;*

- *Method of decision-making;*

- *Post-investment relationships;*

- *Integrity.*

It is clearly imperative if you are entering a business partnership that you have compatible financial objectives – most, but not all, venture capitalists will be looking to make a capital gain on their investment in the medium term (say five years). Examine your own financial objectives carefully and find a compatible partner – don't just parrot: "We are looking for a flotation in three years," if you don't really mean it. It will only lead to grief at a later stage and is largely unnecessary as there are sources of capital with longer-term objectives. Attitudes to dividends vary widely and should be tested. An obvious question to ask, but often forgotten, is: "Does the venture capitalist have the funds available to support your deal not only now, but also in the future?" This will obviously be of much greater importance if acquisitions are a key ingredient of your strategy. If the venture capitalist has specific sector experience, so much the better as he will be familiar with your industry issues and terminology.

Another factor often overlooked by people seeking venture capital is the method of decision-making and the relationships post-investment. As a director, you will be used to making quick decisions – make sure your venture capital partner can keep pace with you. Also, explore how he is going to get involved post-acquisition – do you want support? Is the venture capitalist capable of giving it? Some venture capitalists like to take a major role as the business moves forward, but most will settle for a non-executive directorship – but it is still worth your while making sure he is going to be value for money. Check out who will take up the non-executive directorship, as this will be the focal point of your longer-term relationship.

Perhaps of greatest importance in the end is business and personal integrity. When you embark on an MBO you will be confident that everything in your business plan will work out reasonably well. Of course, in reality the venture capitalist knows (or he should do!) that things will go wrong from time to time. When they do, you need to be sure that you have chosen a partner who will play fair when things don't go quite according to plan.

FINDING YOUR VENTURE CAPITAL PARTNER

Personal recommendation is usually the best way of finding any new supplier and venture capital is no different. As around 5,000 MBOs have been completed in the UK in the last ten years, there is likely to be a business in your town that has been through the process. Track one down and gain from its experience. Your accountant or lawyer will also almost certainly have experience and should be consulted at an early stage for guidance on who might be the appropriate backer for your deal. If you are not satisfied with, or are unable to use personal recommendations, there are a number of directories that can help. The *British Venture Capital Association (BVCA) Directory of Members* is the best one to start with, as it gives you a brief profile of each firm and what it is looking for.

For much smaller transactions the BVCA also publishes a *Directory of Business Angels*, who specialise at the smaller end of the spectrum – less than £500,000. The BVCA is at: Essex House, 12-13 Essex Street, London WC2R 3AA. Telephone: 0171-240 3846.

MAKING THE APPROACH

If you are thinking of an MBO, before approaching the venture capitalist you must check your legal situation. Ideally, you should have formal board authority before speaking to venture capitalists, but if this is not appropriate then ensure that you do not breach any fiduciary responsibilities. You will need a concise business plan and summary. Make a brief telephone call to the venture capitalist to check he is interested in your type of proposal and then send him the summary. Whatever you do, don't scatter business plans around like confetti. Aim to see three or four venture capital groups who have expressed genuine interest in your plan.

MEETING THE VENTURE CAPITALIST

When you get an appointment with a venture capitalist try and get him to your site if you can, as you will feel more comfortable and he will gain a better impression of your business. Unfortunately, he'll probably insist on the first meeting being at his offices as it is a more economical use of his time. As time will be very limited – plan on no longer than an hour – and you are likely to get only one chance, make sure you present your business in the best light. Have a good summary of the key points and be on top of the numbers. If possible, make sure the key members of the team are with you. The venture capitalist will spend most of the meeting quizzing you on your business, but do try and keep back a little time so you can ask him some questions. Ask for a written proposal and ask for some references so you can talk to other chief executives the firm has worked with. The venture capitalist will be doing lots of due diligence on you, so don't forget to do some on him.

TAKING THE DECISION

If you are running a business of any size and strength you will by now have several proposals from a number of credible venture capitalists, all of which meet your initial decision-making criteria. So how do you choose? At this stage it is worth recalling the opening paragraph and remembering that you are on the verge of a new long-term business relationship. This whole process is a little like marriage – you've been to the disco, eyed up all the potential partners and its time to enter the courtship phase. It comes down, therefore, to how comfortable you feel with individuals and the relationships you are likely to form with them. But don't lose sight of the real objectives, which are to buy the company and make it a successful investment for all concerned.

THE FIRST STEPS OF THE ENGAGEMENT

Once you have decided which venture capitalist to work with, make sure you are clear about who is doing what in the few weeks prior to the marriage ceremony. There are many tasks to be completed – appointing a bank or two, taking personal financial advice, taking insurance advice, pensions advice, property advice, legal advice and accounting advice – to name but a few. There will be many advisers vying for your attention – if only to justify the high level of fees they are going to invoice you for soon after completion – and if you are not careful some may well stray into the territory of others. It is important, therefore, to be absolutely clear with your venture capital partner at the outset about who is leading the transaction. Agree a timetable with him, a list of tasks, key responsibilities and a critical path. Now you've found your venture capital partner, the real fun of courting can begin.

Chapter 4

Points of law

Jonathan Blake, partner and head of the private equity team at S J Berwin & Co. summarises areas of the law of which directors of MBO companies need to be aware at the outset of the transaction

The law places onerous responsibilities on a director with regard to his company. As soon as a director decides to take active steps towards an MBO of his company, or any part of it, he should approach the board. To proceed without doing so would give rise to conflicts of interest which could impede the proper performance of his duties. The board will then consider whether or not it wishes to encourage the MBO. If the board is willing to contemplate an MBO, or at least is prepared to see what sort of offer can be put together, then best practice suggests that the following steps should be taken:

■ *A committee of the board of directors – not including the directors involved in the MBO and including as many non-executive directors as possible – should be formed to consider the MBO. The committee may wish to instruct independent professional and financial advisers;*

■ *The committee should agree with the MBO director what information regarding the company he is at liberty to disclose to his backers;*

■ *The committee should agree procedures as to the director's future conduct and voting on the board of directors of the company, and on how much – if any – of his office time he may spend on the MBO. There may also be other conflicts to address;*

■ *The committee may be authorised by the board to negotiate and agree any heads of agreement with the MBO team and its backers.*

DUTY OF THE BOARD

The board has a duty to act in the best interests of the company, its shareholders and employees and therefore ought not to reject an MBO proposal out of hand. Where the company is a subsidiary or closely controlled, it would be bound to consult its owners on any bona fide offer. If, following any such consultation, the board did not agree to the proposed MBO, there would be little point in proceeding further as an MBO obviously can only take place if the owner agrees to sell. In other cases, the financial advisers to the board may recommend that the target is put up for auction to ensure that the MBO terms represent the best reasonably obtainable.

CONFLICTS OF INTEREST

In some cases, directors or executives proceeding towards an MBO may feel reluctant to disclose their intentions at the outset. This will almost certainly put them at risk of being in breach of their contracts of employment as they face many potential conflicts, including:

■ *They will be under a duty not to disclose confidential information to their backers as this could damage the business of the company and also affect a possible MBO. In short, their own interests may not fully coincide with those of the company;*

■ *They cannot involve any of their colleagues in the MBO or persuade staff to join the buy-out vehicle.*

Some of these conflicts would be resolved if the MBO went ahead; the vendor – in selling the company to the MBO company – would probably accept these breaches. However, if the MBO did not proceed, but the director's involvement later came to light – and if in the meantime any decisions were taken or any information was disclosed which damaged the company – the director could be held personally liable for the damage caused, and/or dismissed. There have been some well-publicised cases which illustrate the serious consequences which can follow from a misuse of confidential information.

POTENTIAL LIABILITY OF AN INVESTOR

The proposed investors in the MBO could also be liable if they came to hold and misuse confidential information of the company when they knew that it was obtained in breach of the director's duties, or if they were inducing executives of the company to breach their contracts of employment.

SHAREHOLDER CONSENT

The Companies Act 1985 provides that the consent of shareholders of a company is required for the sale of ten per cent or more of its net tangible assets, or of assets valued at £100,000 or more, to a director of the company or of its holding company or a person connected with such a director (which may include the MBO company).

LISTED COMPANIES

If the company or its ultimate holding company is listed, the sale of assets may require shareholder approval as a result of its size. "Related party" transactions may also require shareholders' approval under Stock Exchange rules. In addition, the normal provisions of the City Code on Takeovers and Mergers apply to all public companies. The board will need to consider carefully an early announcement of the proposed MBO. The Takeover Code includes certain protections for shareholders of public companies which are the subject of an MBO. In particular:

- *The board should seek independent professional advice as soon as it becomes aware of the possible MBO;*

- *The independent directors and their advisers must be furnished with all information provided by the MBO team to their potential financial backers and such information should also be made available to all other offerors;*

- *The board must circulate its own views on the offer to its shareholders together with the substance of advice given to it by independent advisers (directors who are part of the MBO team should not participate in formulating these views).*

The Stock Exchange and Takeover Code rules restricting dealings in shares by directors and other connected persons will apply both before and after the announcement of the MBO, as will the provisions of Part V of the Criminal Justice Act 1993 (which relate to insider dealing) if they are privy to any unpublished price-sensitive information.

THE DIRECTOR AND HIS NEW COMPANY

In many cases an executive involved in the MBO will become a director of the MBO company. Involvement in the MBO company is likely to be more risky than in the former company. The director will have a number of personal liabilities, even if he is a non-executive or nominee director appointed by his financial backers. These will include liabilities for wrongful trading – if the company incurs liabilities at a time when there is no reasonable prospect that it could avoid going into insolvent liquidation – environmental liabilities, liabilities for indemnities, warranties or personal guarantees given to the investors in the MBO or on an eventual exit.

OTHER LEGAL ISSUES IN A BUY-OUT

ENGAGEMENT LETTERS AND LIMITATION OF LIABILITY

An engagement letter will undoubtedly be entered into with the accountancy firm preparing the accountants' report in respect of the business. It has now become established that the "Big Six" accountancy firms will seek to cap their own liability in this engagement letter at £25m, or the value of the deal, if lower. It is also now the practice for these firms to limit their liability on a proportional basis with regard to any claim. If it is only possible for the financial backers of the MBO to recover part of any claim from the accountants, the extent to which the MBO directors are exposed will need to be carefully addressed in the legal documentation.

CAN THE COMPANY UNDERWRITE ABORTIVE LEGAL FEES?

There is a general prohibition on target companies giving financial assistance to the MBO company on its acquisition of the target's shares. It would clearly be unlawful financial assistance for the company whose shares are being purchased to bear the costs of its management in a successful MBO. However, in practice, if the MBO proceeds, fees are likely to be borne by the MBO vehicle. Even where the company is asked to underwrite legal fees on an abortive attempt to purchase its own shares there may be financial assistance issues, and listed companies must also ensure that they do not breach restrictions upon the giving of "exceptional" indemnities without shareholder approval. In all cases the directors should seek advice.

SECURITY FOR DEBT FINANCE

Private companies are, in certain circumstances, able to give financial assistance for an acquisition of their own shares using the assets of the target company as security for the borrowings of the MBO vehicle, and in the vast majority of cases the bank which provides the debt finance will require such security to be given. This will be possible if the directors of the target company are able to make a statutory declaration – backed up by an auditor's letter saying that they are not aware of anything indicating that the directors' opinion is unreasonable – that, in their opinion, the company will be able to pay its debts as they fall due during the year following the MBO. If the giving of security involves any reduction in the net assets of the subsidiary – which will be the case if there is any realistic prospect of the security being called – and, as a result, provision has to be made in its accounts, the amount of that reduction would need to be covered by distributable profits of the company. Public companies cannot give financial assistance but it is sometimes possible for them to re-register as private companies prior to, or following, the MBO and for the security arrangements to be entered into then.

The making of loans by the target company after the buy-out to assist the MBO vehicle in repaying, or paying interest on, the loan incurred for the purpose of the buy-out is also financial assistance – and requires a similar procedure to be undertaken. This does not apply to the payment of dividends by the target company which can only be made out of distributable profits.

Chapter 5

Valuation, negotiation and structure

PART ONE: THE THEORY

Ian Hawkins, partner, Phildrew Ventures, offers tips for mastering the key ingredients of an MBO

Purchasing a company can be compared with purchasing a house. The negotiation process must ultimately present the vendor with an acceptable price, just as the purchaser must be happy that the price offered represents good value – enabling appropriate returns on investment to be made. The concept that the "right" price is that upon which the vendor and purchaser can agree is a truism, but what influences pricing and valuation decisions? Most transactions hit a number of decision points where they proceed or lapse, mostly on the grounds of price.

SUBSIDENCE?

The reasons for sale can have a significant bearing on the negotiation process and the price payable. Just as a tenant may know the good and bad points of a house, so management is usually in the best position to recognise the attractions of purchasing the business it manages. However, management suffers from conflicts of interest when attempting an MBO, the resolution of which determines the nature of subsequent negotiations. Loyalties become divided: on the one hand buy-out management teams should pursue self-interest and negotiate for the lowest possible purchase price by exploiting their knowledge; on the other, they should remember that they are negotiating with shareholders, ultimately their employers, whose interests they are expected to represent and with whom relationships may have to be maintained – either because the sale falls through or because of trading relationships which subsequently survive the transaction. In these circumstances the importance of working with experienced venture capital funding sources and advisers cannot be over-emphasised, and the earlier they are involved the better. Their involvement can protect management from the worst of the conflicts and can encourage the vendor to appreciate the advantages of giving management first option rather than pursuing an expensive auction process. Fees can be saved, the sale can be discreet and avoid exposure of business details to competitors and – because of inside knowledge – deals can be completed quickly at good prices.

FOOT IN THE DOOR

At the first inkling that a parent is likely to consider selling a company, management should put down a marker. An initial approach to a venture capital house is best made with parental approval. The key to success at this point is flexibility to structure the deal to address the vendor's sensitivities and requirements quickly and discreetly.

As information starts to flow and statistics pile up, all sides will be seeking to identify pricing parameters. Views will be formed on what should be an acceptable price based upon the vendor's position, his need for cash, the impact on his earnings and the value of the target company to any other potential competing bidders.

At the same time, the venture capitalist will form initial views of what is affordable, based upon the financial information available, both historic and projected, the attractions of the target company, its products, markets and management. These all combine to paint a picture from which he can anticipate his funding structure and the returns available subject to achieving projected performance. He will also rapidly form a view of what return is required for the level of risk being assumed.

PRICING MODEL

Simplistically, the funding structure and pricing is driven by determining the maximum level of funding available from each source:

■ *Debt is determined by asset backing, cash-flow and the ability to pay interest and make repayments within a sensible timescale;*

- *Equity is predominately sourced from the venture capitalist who will build his return around a mix of income, capital repayment – if cash-flows allow – and capital gain. The mix of ordinary shares and other instruments gear up management's equity interest disproportionately to its cash contribution, but that percentage is predominately driven by the return requirements of the venture capitalist.*

Take the example of a company that is to be sold debt-free with the following profile:

£000's	Latest Historical	Year 1 Forecast	Year 2 Forecast	Year 3 Forecast
Turnover	20,000	22,000	24,000	26,000
Operating profits	2,000	2,200	2,400	2,600
Net assets	13,000			

Net assets are made up of a mix of, say, fixed assets of £8m, trade debtors of £8m and creditors of £3m, ie. net working capital of £5m. Cash-flows approximately match operating profits with capital expenditure matching depreciation.

Senior debt might cost some two per cent over LIBOR (say nine per cent per annum for simplicity) and should be covered at least twice by first year profits. This would indicate a maximum debt package in the order of £10m. Above this level the banks would possibly question the asset backing and the ability to repay (typically over seven years). If the pricing estimate is, say, £17m, a total equity package around £8m would be required, leaving around £1m to cover the costs of the transaction and some working capital contingency. The equity would be made up of some £1m in ordinary shares and £7m in preference shares or subordinated debt. Management might subscribe for 20 per cent of the ordinary shares and the venture capitalist provide the balance, by way of £800,000 of ordinary shares and £7m of preference shares.

If the company is sold after three years for £26m, ie. ten times operating profits, this could be shared out as follows:

	£000's
Offer price	26,000
Repay outstanding debt	(7,000)
Redeem preference shares with 10 per cent p.a. return	(9,317)
Available to ordinary shares	9,683
Split:	
Management – 20 per cent	1,937
Venture capitalist – 80 per cent	7,746
	9,683

Thus management turns £200,000 into £1.9m and the venture capitalist £7.8m into £17.1m – a return of 30 per cent per annum. However, the assumptions made might not allow so much debt or such high returns and the structuring process must be rejuggled by an iterative process until the mix of the purchase price, debt levels, realisation assumptions and returns all balance.

NEGOTIATING WITH THE VENDOR

Having confirmed some interest in a sale and persuaded a venture capitalist to join forces, management is ready to enter negotiation. Price will be the major consideration and it would be usual to indicate a range which has, at its top end, the figure emerging from the pricing model. This assumes all good news and few contingencies. Management may only get one shot at an exclusive bid and needs to put its best foot forward to avoid the vendor seeking other bids to ensure it does its duty to secure the best price. If the indication price is in the right "ball-park" the haggling ensues. Price tends to make way for comfort factors and management can gain advantage by being willing to take problems – which it can understand and quantify – off the vendor's hands. These problems, such as a loss making subsidiary or an exposure to some historic event, may put off competing bidders.

In many instances the vendor will have a need to secure a headline price which cannot readily be justified. In this case the vendor will often be offered some deferred consideration or a residual stake. In the example above, the vendor might retain a 25 per cent stake (ie. one third of the venture capitalist's stake) receiving a net figure of £15.5m, ie. £18m less one third of £7.75m, for apparently selling 75 per cent of the company, implying a valuation of almost £21m versus the £18m above. Alternatively, the deferred consideration may only be payable when a future event or performance benchmark has occurred which helps justify the higher price.

DUE DILIGENCE

Eventually the management team should seek to secure agreement in principle and an exclusivity period during which it is able to investigate the company and complete the transaction without fear of being "gazumped" by another offer. The results of due diligence may allow the offer to be confirmed, but possibly with conditions attached – and this may generate further negotiation. If significant problems are identified the offer price may be revised – the parallel being with a house survey.

COMPLETION

The process culminates, after several weeks, in a completion meeting at which all elements of the transaction are pulled together. Despite significant preparation, negotiations often continue until all documents are signed and all disclosures made, most compromises being made after midnight! In the aftermath of completion, the Champagne flows and all thoughts of pricing and negotiation fade. Management has secured its own independent castle until its "exit" looms when management and venture capitalists themselves become vendors, seeking maximum valuation, via a trade sale or alternatively by stepping up to become a quoted company.

PART TWO: THE PRACTICE

Barry Hannington, managing director, RVP Foods recalls the pain and the pleasure of the sale of Ross Vegetable Products

In early 1996 United Biscuits decided to sell off Ross Vegetable Products, its frozen vegetable products division. Initially as managing director, I assisted the vendor in preparing the company for sale. But, when news came that a number of the bids submitted were contingent on my continued appointment, everything changed.

I joined the Ross Group food company in 1954 when it was still a family-run business. Over the next 42 years, I helped to grow and develop the business as it changed hands a number of times, and in 1996, led a £50m management buy-out of Ross Vegetable Products from its owner, United Biscuits.

United Biscuits bought the company from Hanson in 1988 and integrated it into its own frozen and chilled food business. But by the early nineties the division had begun to struggle as the market became crowded by smaller entrepreneurial competitors. Over a three-year period, United Biscuits reorganised its frozen and chilled foods operations into four distinct business units. In 1995, the Ross Vegetable Products business unit achieved a turnover of £56.1m and operating profits of £6.2m.

But a further cut in costs was needed. So at the end of that year we disbanded UB Ross Young's and created three separate businesses, making substantial savings by reducing the head count, including five board directors, by ten per cent. I was appointed managing director of the frozen vegetable and ready-made meals subsidiary, which included green vegetables, vegetable mixes and ready-made meals under the Ross Oriental Express brand.

Soon after, however, the parent company advised me of its plans to sell the business. Over the next four rather hectic months, I put together a new management team, fine-tuned the business strategy and began briefing consultants Arthur Andersen, who had been instructed to identify potential buyers.

Arthur Andersen produced a short list of trade buyers, another of international buyers and a further list of institutional buyers. In all, I showed at least eight different groups of prospective bidders around our two factories and presented my vision for the future of the business to each in turn. Much of the hard work that was needed to turn the business around was already under way.

When the bids came in, three out of four were conditional on my staying at the helm. I knew that the company had a very promising future and agreed, on the understanding that I could negotiate a satisfactory departure from United Biscuits.

From that moment onwards, my situation changed completely. I now knew what it was like to chaperoned for much of my working day. Three accountants came and sat in my outer office for about 12 weeks as part of due diligence. An important, but quite tricky, part of my job was to co-operate with the auditors. I was permitted to receive telephone calls and make pertinent observations, but if any of my comments were likely to have a derogatory effect on the purchasers' value of the business, I had to seek approval before I could comment.

It was only in the final quarter of the proceedings that we got down to the detailed work of the management bid itself. Up until then we had been preoccupied with implementing the new business strategy which involved selecting an advertising agent, working up a media campaign and preparing for a complete relaunch of the Ross Oriental Express Meals core range, scheduled for early 1997.

However smoothly the MBO process runs, there will inevitably be points when it looks as though the negotiations are going to fold. It is at these crucial moments that someone who knows the business intimately can step into the breach.

The crucial "summit" meeting, where we finally exchanged contracts took place in London on a grey December day. We arrived at the offices of Clifford Chance at 9.30 in the morning where our negotiations were among many similar such deal-making sessions going on that day. In the beginning I was pretty confident that we would be finished by 6.30pm at the latest, but the process actually lumbered along extremely slowly.

By about 5.00pm, the negotiations seemed to be getting nowhere and I was beginning to despair. There were now only about nine points still awaiting resolution. In the end I approached one of the vendor's representatives – a former colleague of mine – and suggested that he and I have a crack at sorting it out ourselves, well away from the lawyers. This worked out well, and at last we were able to move forward. Each of us then told our respective lawyers what changes were needed. After that we had to wait while the contracts were retyped.

Our deal is an example of what has become known as an institutional buy-out. Backed by Phildrew Ventures, my new company RVP Foods paid United Biscuits £44m in cash, £2m of which was deferred and paid by installments over an 18-month period. A further £6m was retained for expansion and modernising the plant. Eventually the deal was concluded at 3.30am. I was then driven back to Newark and had just enough time to shave before I went into the factory at North Thoresby in Lincolnshire, to tell the staff that we had bought the business and formed a company called RVP Foods. I then drove 90 miles to deliver this very same news in person to our factory personnel at Fakenham, in Norfolk.

Having worked in a corporate environment for over 40 years, it took me a little time to adjust to independent company life, but I am constantly delighted by the fact that I am judged solely on what the company does. I can decide on the strategy and development and when and where to invest. We have already invested £2m at our Fakenham factory where we are installing high speed packing and weighing equipment. In addition, we shall have invested almost £4m in the media and promotional plans we have for this year.

Presently we are turning over £60m and producing 25 million meals a year. Our output is split exactly in half between private label products and our own brands. My focus now is to grow the company by increasing sales of our branded products. As well as managing the business day-by-day we are working on the longer-term, to shape the company so that we can float it on the stockmarket in three years' time.

Chapter 6

The need for independent advice

Chris Ward, head of private equity at Deloitte & Touche corporate finance, advises on how to choose good independent advisers and highlights what they can bring to your buy-out

If you think you can lead a buy-out without help from professional advisers, just stop for a moment to consider what will be required of you during the process:

- *Drafting and presenting business plans that promote you and your company;*

- *Responding to detailed questioning on all aspects of the business and its operations; questions initially from prospective equity investors and banks, but later on from investigating accountants;*

- *Negotiating terms with your financial backers;*

- *Negotiating with the vendor and the vendor's agents;*

- *Dealing with your customers, employees, suppliers and customers; AND*

- *Running your company!*

All this sounds somewhat daunting, and it is. But the right advisers can help manage and co-ordinate the process, reducing the risk of you being distracted from running the business. Furthermore, an independent adviser will be just that: independent from the vendor and from the financiers. So you, the management, know exactly whose side he or she is on – yours.

Bearing in mind that this is likely to be your first experience of a buy-out, how do you choose a financial adviser and what in particular should you be looking for?

EXPERIENCE

Don't take risks by retaining advisers who are unfamiliar with buy-outs. Examine their track record and experience. Ask them to provide you with the names of buy-out clients they have previously advised, and take references – both for deals that have been completed and deals that have been aborted. (Do not believe them if they say that they have never had an aborted deal.)

THE TEAM

Check who will do the work. Beware the sales team who tell a good story but who are never to be seen again.

CHEMISTRY

Are your advisers enthusiastic about working with you? Do you like them? Do they inspire your confidence? Other things being equal, don't be afraid to follow your instincts.

FEES

Be clear about the basis on which your adviser proposes to charge, and obtain fee estimates. Good advice rarely comes cheap, and the full costs of an MBO will be beyond the means of most management teams. However, this should not be a stumbling block. Transaction costs will be met out of the finance raised for the buy-out. Some fees, such as those of the reporting accountants, will be underwritten by the financiers and in any event most financial advisers are prepared to work for management wholly or mainly on a success (no deal, no fee) basis.

You may have found advisers who have the relevant experience, who you like, who are keen to help you and who are available. But you must now check precisely what they propose to do and what value they will add to your transaction. You should expect them to provide assistance in a number of ways.

FEASIBILITY ASSESSMENT

This is the first stage, and in many ways the most important. You need to be advised on whether the buy-out can be financed at a price that is likely to be acceptable to the vendor. That advice should be objective and your advisers should have no vested interests beyond ensuring that you are properly advised.

Your advisers should spend time with you and your team to obtain a good understanding of your business, the key issues that affect it, the markets in which it operates, your customers and your competition. They should critically review your business plan and financial projections, advise on how this might be strengthened and prepare you for meetings with potential investors. Your advisers should know what kinds of businesses are "backable" and what issues are likely to be of interest to financiers.

An important ingredient in the feasibility assessment is an outline valuation of your business from which an initial financing structure for the buy-out can be developed. Anticipating and discussing issues that might be "deal-breakers" is another: early identification of factors that can mitigate potential problems will increase your chances of success.

Above all, your adviser will need to understand your personal as well as corporate objectives if you are to be properly advised on the structuring and financing of your buy-out. The feasibility assessment should provide you with the reliable answers to your key questions:

- *What can we afford to pay?*

- *What will we as management have to invest personally?*

- *How much equity will we get?*

INFORMATION MEMORANDUM

Your advisers should help you prepare an information memorandum, which will draw on your existing business plan and will provide sufficient relevant information in an appropriate way to attract investor interest. The contents of this document will vary depending upon the nature and sector of your business, but may well include sections covering:

- *Executive summary;*

- *Background to the transaction/history of the company;*

- *Products, services and competition;*

- *Markets and marketing;*

- *Management and personnel;*

- *Risk factors and rewards;*

- *Financial information.*

FINANCIAL STRUCTURING AND TAX PLANNING

Your advisers should devise an outline capital structure, which meets your personal and corporate objectives and which will be acceptable to potential investors. They would consider the relevant accounting issues and advise on efficient tax structuring of the buy-out.

The right financial structure for your buy-out is one which accommodates the needs of the business and which allows not only for all the transaction costs, but also for future capital expenditure and working capital requirements, and takes into account your preferences as to the most appropriate method and timing of your exit. You should expect your advisers to steer you away from a structure which would force you to take uncommercial short-term decisions simply to satisfy the terms of financiers; your advisers should be focused on achieving the best possible deal for you, consistent with your longer-term objectives.

RAISING CAPITAL

Turning the outline financial structure into a reality is definitely the job of your financial adviser. An experienced adviser with a good knowledge of the finance market should be able to select those financial institutions with a real appetite for your transaction, and then arrange for you and your team to present the buy-out opportunity to them formally. It is not cheating for them to rehearse you and prepare you for difficult questions!

Independent advisers have no investment funds under management and therefore no conflicts of interest, so can offer impartial advice on the terms offered by financiers. In doing so, they should take into account all the relevant financial terms, but also advise you on the less obvious non-financial factors. You should therefore expect your advisers to advise you in respect of your equity stake; how much you should be investing for that stake; your remuneration package and service contract; the restrictions that may be placed on you post buy-out; financial covenants, and so on. You want your advisers to negotiate the most attractive financial package for you, which may not necessarily be the one that provides management with the highest stake on day one.

VENDOR NEGOTIATIONS

There has to be a willing seller in any buy-out, and your financial advisers should advise on negotiation strategy. You may also wish them to negotiate on your behalf so as to preserve your relationship with the vendor. They should help you determine the main areas of negotiating strength and how to derive maximum benefit from these; it is equally important to identify negotiating weaknesses so that these can be addressed and minimised or marginalised where possible.

Just as there are important non-financial considerations to be taken into account in raising capital, so is the case when negotiating with the vendor. In a buy-out, management's weakness may be the constraint on the price that can be bid – that price must be within the capacity of the new stand-alone entity to service and repay the external finance.

However, the management team's strongest cards are often the speed with which it can progress, the confidentiality that can be maintained during the process and the flexibility of the structure which, for instance, can allow for the vendor to retain a stake in the business. Your advisers should be experienced and successful negotiators, who will make the most use of non-price issues.

PROJECT MANAGEMENT

Your time is precious, and you must continue to devote some of it to running the business. Your advisers should ensure that you nevertheless retain control and influence over the course of the transaction. They should:

- *Structure timetables and co-ordinate the various professionals, supporting you and highlighting priorities;*

- *Liaise with the lawyers to ensure that the important features of the transaction are properly reflected in the legal documentation;*

- *Advise you on how to finance your own investment;*

- *Provide you with personal tax advice.*

POST BUY-OUT

By the time you get to completion, you and your team will have worked very hard and will deserve the celebration party. But there is life after a buy-out! You will now be required to deliver on your business plan and ultimately achieve an exit for your investors. In fact, the really hard work starts now.

By this time, your advisers should know you very well, should understand the issues facing you and your business, and should be keen to help you achieve your goals. If you are similarly keen to maintain the relationship, this will at least tell you that you chose the right advisers in the first place.

Chapter 7

The bank relationship

Graham Randell, managing director of NatWest Markets acquisition finance, stresses the importance of building a strong long-term relationship

The initial meeting with the banker is an important stage, with both sides looking to make a strong first impression. This will form the basis of a long-term relationship. Personal chemistry on both sides is extremely important as many hours will be spent together while the transaction progresses through to completion.

It is essential that all involved have a clear understanding of the business of the other parties and of the risks involved in a buy-out, as the procedure is a highly controlled affair.

PLANNING AND STRATEGY

Most importantly management should recognise a buy-out as a real opportunity, and have a clear and concise sense of strategic direction when presenting its business plan. This will help to secure investor confidence in the team and its proposal. The management team should be guided by its professional advisers who will be able to direct it to backers whose investment criteria are most likely to match the financial requirements of the MBO team. They may also suggest that the various financial players are put into a 'beauty parade' to ensure that they obtain the best deal possible.

A well-managed business will always gain the support and commitment of its banker. A professional and experienced bank will always be able to devote the necessary time to complete a sophisticated transaction swiftly as it will have the resources to meet management's needs if required. It will also be able to be in contact with key decision-makers. Securing a good relationship is always a key factor and it may be that the most competitive offer with regards to the management's share of the buy-out vehicle, or the keenest margins on senior debt, will not represent the best choice.

Likewise the bankers should show management their commitment by demonstrating their understanding of, and enthusiasm for, the business. Information flows during a management buy-out process can seem demanding, but it makes sense for all parties to be as open as possible. Banks tend not to like unwelcome surprises. Allowing a bank to do its business, ie. analyse all the risks presented to it, is a better way to create the relationship than not highlighting all the risks.

HOW DO YOU ACCESS THE BANK DEBT?

Generally, although a bank is looking for a satisfactory return, its primary concern will be for the security of funds it is advancing. Thus, it is important for the buy-out team and its professional advisers to prepare carefully a proposal to be presented to the intended financial backers with this point in mind.

Bankers will do their homework before attending a meeting and will have a list of issues to clarify before leaving. Among the issues listed on a banker's agenda, integrity and track record will be high in the order of priorities. Management's ability to obtain bank finance will depend on the lender's ability to investigate closely the quality of the team's marketing, technical and financial ability and its creditworthiness. If there has been a failed bid previously, a bank will know this prior to the meeting. It is thus even more important for the borrower to be able to persuade and convince the lender that the deal in its current structure is going to succeed.

In the current MBO climate, the market is flooded with aggressive debt providers to finance a proposal. However, when choosing a financier it is important that a good reputable bank with experience, resource and capability is able to fund the transaction. Banks with experience in the market place will be competitive, responsive and flexible in providing other forms of finance to support a business's normal requirements.

Once a suitable funding partner is chosen, the lender will go through an intense process to make absolutely sure that its risk is minimal. A timetable will need to be established to ensure that all parties are meeting the same deadlines. Concentrated analysis will then enable the lender to decide how much debt the company can obtain and at what price.

A business plan will need to be prepared by management which will also test its ability to forecast information and the adequacy of the cash-flow. Prime focus will be on earnings, cash-flow and capital backing. Subsequent meetings will be held to discuss all the issues emanating from the business plan, after which the banker will need to visit the company's sites so that he can validate the business plan by understanding the operations and functions of the enterprise.

The due diligence report will provide a rigorous analysis of, and commentary on, many aspects of the business. It is a major tool used by banks to analyse the company and certainly aids the decision in providing the debt. Some businesses will require a separate market report depending on which industry they are in. The report is compiled by an industry specialist and will cover every aspect of the market.

Having formed an initial 'feel' for the proposition and established that the purpose of the loan is acceptable, the banker will turn his attention to the likely return for the risk. However, not until all aspects of the transaction have been calculated will the pricing be settled.

HOW MUCH DEBT SHOULD YOU HAVE?

Senior debt will generally represent the main source of acquisition funding and is usually the cheapest form of institutional finance available to the management team. Therefore the view may be that debt should be maximised before turning to equity. Any additional funding required can be made up by a combination of equity and mezzanine debt. Mezzanine sits between senior debt and equity and displays characteristics of both. While it is interest-bearing in nature, increased risks relative to senior debt entitle it to a share in the equity return, usually via an attached warrant. Companies whose cash-flows are cyclical usually also require working capital facilities to fund their operations.

Habitually, the first step will be to decide how much senior debt can be raised to support the purchase price. There is no book of rules to follow to determine the answer. Nevertheless certain assumptions are made. Ensuring that the management team is good enough plays a major part. The stability of earnings is another important factor which determines the target company's cash-flow and the level of debt. The bank will also request the target company to prove that any profit improvements are sustainable, based on demonstrable savings and rationalisation. The company's ability to borrow may also be extended if it has a market niche and diversity of customers. Other points to look at in a management buy-out company would be the extent to which the company can be sub-divided into discrete operations or assets and also the quality of assets, particularly current assets.

Once the borrower has established the amount that can be borrowed, debt providers need to be content that the debt can be repaid, normally within a five to seven year period. In some cases repayment can be "back-ended" so that allowance for a capital expenditure programme can be made.

When banking capital is plentiful, margins are tightened, fees reduced, more highly leveraged structures are created and terms are longer. One understandable reaction to the leverage concept is that lots of debt equates to lots of risk, and surely it would be better to achieve a more conservative balance? Risk is inevitable in an MBO, and a struggling buy-out can turn into an unpleasant experience for all. However, the level of debt is unlikely to be the sole cause of failure; it is more likely to accelerate the process of demise (or success). Consequently, the bank will take a reasonable set of "base case" projections, sensitise them for a range of events working against the company and then want to be reasonably satisfied that the loan can be serviced and repaid, factoring in all the above criteria. It is this adjusted case (the sensitivities) that will determine the level of funding that a bank will be prepared to extend to a transaction.

A lender will also want to be satisfied that there is prudent asset coverage and that his covenant risk (ie. the likelihood of a company being unable to service its debt) is low. A widely used measure is interest cover. The bank, as a rule of thumb, would like to see interest covered by operating profits by at least twice in year one, with incremental increases thereafter. Furthermore, it will also look to see that the operating cash-flow cover is comfortable and the company has the ability to service costs from revenues. Essentially, cash is king and the due diligence investigations are designed to address the cash-generating ability of the new venture. It is against the results of these further inquiries that the decision of how much to lend is made.

THE ONGOING RELATIONSHIP

The deal is done and it is now the first day in the life of the new company. The relationship between management and banker has been formed in a series of long, often late-night meetings, but now that the fee has been paid will the enthusiasm of the banker change? The whole operation of a buy-out needs to be a two-way process to build a good relationship and management should seek a bank that reflects what its idea of a relationship should be, not just in the initial phase, but also when the deal has been done. Over the weeks leading up to finalisation of the deal, relationships will be formed and management should ask which of these parties will still be around should help be needed to manage unforeseen events.

If one accepts the adage of banking being a service industry – "a people business" – then management should always be certain that it is talking to people who it can trust and with whom it can forge a long-term association. It is expensive to seek to change at a later date and getting it right at the outset will ensure a successful partnership approach. To sum up with an old adage:

"Beware of the banker that lends you an umbrella
when the sun is shining but takes it away when it rains".

Thinking small? Keep thinking. We're more interested in anyone considering an **MBO** or **MBI** of £10m or more. That's what we call a big deal. And with funds totalling over £400m as well as over 60 such transactions under our belt, we've the necessary clout to put your deal together. So you see, thinking small is not our line. Give us a call and we can start thinking big.

PHILDREW VENTURES

Creative Capital for Management Buy-Outs

PHILDREW VENTURES, TRITON COURT, 14 FINSBURY SQUARE, LONDON EC2A 1PD. TEL 0171 628 6366

Key issue: Specialist production technique, such as forging titanium heads for golf clubs.

Due diligence response: Check process is well-documented. Check key managers are tied to the business contractually, well-remunerated and covered by key man insurance.

Key issue: Security of supplies, such as mineral extraction rights.

Due diligence response: Check contractual position. Assess balance of relationship between the parties; if it is too one-sided, the counter-party may be motivated to break the contract.

Key issue: Relationship with customers, such as fast-moving consumer goods supplied to retailers.

Due diligence response: Examine correspondence, especially contract negotiations, to understand customer requirements, covering reliability of service and product innovation as well as merely price; also understand likely trend of development in these attributes. Check that target business is complying with contractual arrangements covering, for example, merchandising and marketing support. Evaluate the balance of the relationship between the parties.

Key issue: Management skill, such as deployment of assets for hire.

Due diligence response: Understand the trend of developments in the market being served. Check that key managers are tied to the business contractually, well-remunerated and covered by key man insurance.

The list of potential problems is longer and more depressing. Again, I will illustrate the areas which can cause concern with a few examples:

Key issue: Natural disasters, such as fire at factory or warehouse premises.

Due diligence response: Check effectiveness and adequacy for insurance cover, including consequential loss.

Key issue: Environmental damage caused, for example, by vehicle maintenance facilities.

Due diligence response: Check procedures for dealing with leaks and spills. Assess reports of recent incidents. Consider need for physical survey of site. Evaluate potential clean-up costs.

Key issue: Pension and post-retirement benefit, obligations of automotive component supplier, with workforce reduced through automation.

Due diligence response: Understand the basis of the liability, both contractual and other. Check calculation of actuarial liability.

Key issue: Aggressive tax planning schemes in existence.

Due diligence response: Evaluate open issues and their probable outcome, including those which have yet to be considered by tax authorities.

Key issue: Litigation, such as disputes over trading contracts.

Due diligence response: Examine correspondence concerning disputes to identify those which may be difficult to settle. Evaluate open issues in the light of legal advice.

Key issue: Long-term contracts, such as civil engineering contractor.

Due diligence response: Understand costing and bidding procedures. Review contracts in progress to identify those which are off track. Evaluate costs of completion for those contracts where losses in future seem probable.

One of the signal advantages of an MBO is that the resident management probably has the best idea of the problems which the business can face. It is never safe to ignore something which managers themselves identify as a significant issue.

Equally, it is vital to check their list against one based on broader business experience, in case there is something they have missed which could represent a serious threat. This aspect of the due diligence process can be very downbeat; it is a matter of hunting for skeletons.

SYSTEMATIC RISK MANAGEMENT

The positive side of it is in understanding how management measures and controls the threats which it regards as significant. A problem which management has foreseen and which, when it arises, it meets with a planned response, is much less likely to do serious damage. The areas which would normally be covered by this process include:

- *Asset protection, such as ownership and security of premises;*

- *Stock control, both security and minimising the cash locked up;*

- *Supply chain management, ensuring that the information systems minimise working capital requirements and maximise customer service;*

- *Internal controls, to minimise the risk of misappropriation of funds; this area should also cover treasury management and tax planning;*

- *People management, to ensure staff are working for the company not for its downfall.*

PUTTING THEORY INTO PRACTICE

The examples I have used in this chapter are fairly simple and straightforward. I do not want to leave you with the impression that the due diligence process is all about putting ticks in boxes to ensure that every significant issue has been covered and can be safely ignored. In the real world, issues are complex and require sophisticated judgement. For some items it may simply not be possible to reach any conclusion with a reasonable degree of certainty. In such cases, the outcome of the due diligence is a negotiating brief for the MBO team and their financial backers to agree with the vendor how the risk is to be shared between them, and whether any price adjustment is required.

In summary, the ideal outcome of a due diligence exercise is that the risks and opportunities are well-understood by the buying side. Plans can then be put in place so that opportunities are exploited to the greatest possible extent and, through planning and contractual arrangements, downside risks are kept within reasonable bounds. Finally, I never said it was easy. If it were, most of the high-powered army of professionals presently engaged in due diligence work would be employed elsewhere.

PART TWO: THE PAIN

David Gravells, chairman of the Greetings Store Group, gives a warts-and-all account of due diligence

From a base of 11 greetings card and gift stores in West Yorkshire, purchased in November 1994, the Greetings Store Group was, by late 1996, poised to buy two national companies. This would bring the total number of stores to over 200, and establish us as the third largest specialist retail chain in this sector. The deal was in effect a reverse takeover of two larger companies by a much smaller one. Clearly, a favourable due diligence report was essential to secure final approval for the funding. For the management team, the credibility of our plans was at stake in a deal which was already very complex.

ART OR SCIENCE?

The fieldwork undertaken by the accountants required the diverting of limited resources, both within our relatively small company, and the target companies – one of which had been in administration for eight months. The administrator was willing to allow them considerable access but difficulties were caused by his own ad-hoc accounting system: no audit of the previous year's statutory accounts had taken place and management accounts had not been prepared during the period of administration. The vendors of the second target company, while it was the subject of an agreed deal, were inevitably less willing to allow extensive disruption of their operations. Consequently the task of obtaining the necessary data was made much more difficult. This was further complicated by significant inter-group transactions which were not easy to understand, together with inadequate historical management accounts. Because of the accountants' difficulty in obtaining what they perceived as complete and accurate data, there was a tendency to push back to management the gathering of information necessary to resolve these issues and to ask us to do further, more detailed due diligence than we perhaps felt was necessary.

The accountants' first report was actually produced very quickly and acknowledged in general terms that our strategy of bringing together three businesses into one tightly controlled entity, with the benefits of reduced overheads, better purchasing power and improved margins, had validity. However, as always, the devil was in the detail. The initial report contained an enormous number of what the management team felt to be misunderstandings, misinterpretations and misinformation. It was, of course, relatively easy to correct some of the simple inaccuracies although we were frequently surprised at the number of occasions on which straightforward information had been misrepresented, albeit unintentionally.

PROCEED WITH CAUTION

The need to validate our plans to the accountants' satisfaction required a prodigious amount of re-working of the figures, not only to justify profit and loss and funds-flow projections, but also in altering sensitivities. Disagreement arose over fundamental issues such as likely sales figures. Not only did we feel we had been cautious in the first place, but our continued experience throughout the period of due diligence demonstrated that. Against a background of a multitude of meetings with the vendor, corporate finance advisers, lawyers, property consultants and bankers, and the managing of our own business in an efficient and effective way – in case the deal did not progress, for whatever reason – the time pressures were incredibly demanding.

Aside from matters which were familiar to management, there were also some very specific disagreements about accountancy principles and standards. As a result, an enormous amount of time and money was spent in detailed conversations about the treatment of matters such as depreciation and goodwill especially in respect of a fair value for store fixed assets, taxation and contingent liabilities for property costs under privity of contract. These often developed into arguments between different groups of professional advisers, with the management team in the frustrating position of watching these lengthy discussions take place, without resolution, while the fees and associated costs continued to rack up.

Some of the most irritating issues arose around nuances of words and phrases. For management, conscious of the need to ensure the overall report was as positive in tone as possible when it was read by the venture capitalists, the banks and other interested parties, expressions such as "should be able to overcome the problem", "loss-making businesses" and "imprudence" took on considerable significance. Often the accountants seemed to use unnecessarily robust descriptions of situations or issues which had been recognised by us and where we had already indicated what action we intended to take to rectify the problem.

FOUR PIECES OF ADVICE:

- *Never underestimate the amount of time necessary to devote to due diligence. As far as is practical, ensure management's own due diligence is as detailed and as wide in scope as possible, anticipating the questions of the reporting accountants;*

- *In addition to the base case in a thoroughly well-prepared business plan, acknowledge the inevitable cultural approach of the accountants and prepare, in advance, plans with different sensitivities;*

- *Ensure that the initial draft report is produced as quickly as possible. This will allow the maximum amount of time to discuss and argue the changes that are felt appropriate;*

- *Try and keep control of the costs: ask why any and every item of due diligence is being done and for who's benefit. Who actually wants or needs it?*

FINAL WORD

It is fair to say that throughout our due diligence process all the people involved were unfailingly courteous, professional and willing to be as helpful as possible within their own parameters. "No pain, no gain!" A cliché? Of course, but still true in this and, I suspect, most such major, ultimately successful acquisitions.

Chapter 9

Institutional buy-outs

Martin Thorp, European head of corporate finance, and Chris Rowlands, head of private equity, UK corporate finance at Arthur Andersen explain why IBOs are emerging as an attractive alternative to the more traditional MBO/MBI

So what is an institutional buy-out (IBO)? A simple and purist description is where an institution acquires a majority control of a business while conducting the negotiations as principal. In present market conditions this will often be in competition with trade buyers and other financial buyers. The process will usually involve a vendor-conducted auction process, either self-managed or through an accounting firm or merchant bank intermediary.

Given the very significant amounts of capital raised by funds specialising in leveraged transactions throughout the UK and Europe, the concept of a financial buyer conducting an IBO has gained a new level of credibility for vendors contemplating a disposal – both in terms of price and "deliverability". Compared with the way in which some vendors have historically frowned upon the MBO – for its financial fragility and suspicions surrounding management conflicts – the trend towards IBOs may be unlocking opportunities for participation by management teams in deals from which they might otherwise have been excluded.

In practice, there are variations in institutional investment policy that determine whether the institution really is acquiring a business in its own right, or merely continuing to back a management team while taking the high ground in negotiations with the vendor, devising the financial structure and project managing the whole process.

HIGH QUALITY MANAGEMENT ABOUNDS

Many myths abound over institutions that aggressively buy "over the head" of existing management, only to manage the business themselves with total disregard for the position of other stakeholders. In reality, this has rarely happened. Institutions will always want their investee businesses to be run by high quality managers, whether they are to be found among the existing structure, from an injection of fresh and appropriately experienced management from outside or, typically, a combination of the two. With the scale of capital now being mobilised in these transactions, it is not surprising that the institution will require board representation and a close involvement in the development and direction of the company's strategy. In the quoted company arena this would surely not be regarded as unreasonable.

How then does an IBO differ from a more traditional MBO or MBI? The underlying transaction for an IBO would probably be within the leveraged MBO category (ie. transaction consideration in excess of £10m). The term IBO would definitely apply where the transaction size exceeded £100m. The sheer weight of institutional capital that is required to fund such a transaction while maintaining a robust financial structure is likely to result in an institutionally-controlled business, with the management team securing a minority equity stake or some other form of performance-related equity participation. The institution will play a significant part in the strategic direction of the business in terms of its development, and perhaps through subsequent acquisition, flotation and, more significantly, the exit. It is unlikely, therefore, to see a proprietorial or distinctly owner-managed business created from an IBO. By contrast, successful MBOs have historically been capable of repaying the leveraged structure and continuing a dividend flow to the institution, while also maintaining many of the attributes of a privately-held business.

So why has this trend developed? It is possible to trace one route by reference to the original name applying to this type of transaction in its early origins – "the bought deal". In attempting to fend off competition for deal opportunities from other financial institutions and trade bidders, a number of institutions took the then adventurous step of protecting deal-flow by effectively buying the deal. This enabled them to rely far less upon other sources of contributory finance.

THE CHANGING NATURE OF DEAL-FLOW

The dynamics of deal-flow have played an important role in fashioning the trend. The accounting profession became a significant source of leveraged transactions for the venture captial community and, arguably, began to treat the supply of capital as a mere commodity. In response to this, institutions have increasingly sought ways of developing proprietary deal-flow in which they can influence price and terms directly. The power of the cheque book has caused the role of "ringmaster" in a transaction to revert to the institution controlling all aspects such as price negotiation, financial engineering and terms.

Another important factor in the development of the IBO market is the impact on institutional returns. The traditional MBO structure incorporates a significant minority stake for management, and often a controlling position. As competition for these transactions increases from trade buyers and other financial purchasers, the increased weight of institutional capital required to stake a winning bid, supresses the institutional returns, if attractive levels of participation for management are also preserved. Now it could be argued that this places the institution at an unfair advantage over management when negotiating the split of those returns. But through an IBO an institution can invest more capital while maintaining an acceptable level of return. Not only can this result in a more competitive bid, but it is more likely to secure the transaction which otherwise might have been lost to a trade bidder (who would bring uncertainties for management's future as well as lack of participation in the equity).

INSTITUTIONAL FUNDRAISING

The dynamics of institutional fundraising have also influenced the trend towards IBOs. Not only does a history of realised rates-of-return provide a critical credential for raising further funds but the institution's ability to mobilise the capital raised is paramount. Investors typically expect to see their funds invested over a three-year period and in a mature, well-funded marketplace like the UK, opportunities to place large amounts of capital, while maintaining a balance in portfolio exposure, can be hard to find. Again, therefore, this concept of creating and controlling investment opportunities creates a process to meet that need.

Will this trend towards the IBO continue and, if so, what are the implications? From the variety of perspectives discussed, it seems unlikely that management-dominated structures will return to the larger transactions – especially as there are now so many high-calibre and mobile managers who are happy to leave their corporate career to participate in an IBO. However, the best source of due diligence is usually the incumbent management team, whereas in an IBO investment judgements have to be made and decisions taken with little or no access to the existing management. It will be interesting to see just how effective external sources of due diligence can be in supporting quality investment decisions.

FUTURE OPPORTUNITIES

There is frustration with the now standard auction process – where institutions are encouraged to bid against each other. They are tying up a lot of resources and incurring third-party costs. Institutions need innovative ways of generating good IBO opportunities. The less-developed private equity markets in Europe are attractive in this respect and, no doubt, from time to time difficulties in other markets or the economy will create different opportunities. The overall stockmarket performance of the smaller capitalised, quoted companies can sometimes severely limit a company's access to captial. A private equity solution may provide the answer. Economic turbulence could cause the IBO trend to falter, but as the process becomes increasingly robust, it is more likely to be a question of adaptation for the prevailing economic circumstances rather than an absolute decline. We think they are here to stay.

Chapter 10

Buy-outs and tax

Linda Marston-Weston, senior M&A tax manager, Price Waterhouse, advises on the tax implications of buy-outs

In practice, there is likely to be a conflict in the tax objectives of the two main parties to the buy-out: the vendors will want to minimise tax on the disposal, while the purchasers will want a structure that maximises their tax reliefs going forward. To agree a structure acceptable to both, compromises often have to be made.

ACQUISITION STRUCTURE

The most common method of effecting a buy-out is to form a new company (Newco) to make the acquisition. The participating equity of Newco will be held by the management team and the venture capital house (which is likely to hold the majority of the equity); in addition, some lower-tier management may also be able to invest. The acquisition is then likely to follow one of two routes:

■ *Newco could acquire the shares of the target;*

■ *Newco could acquire the trade and assets of the target (or more likely, Newco would set up a wholly-owned operating subsidiary which would acquire the trade and assets).*

In most cases, the preference of the purchaser will be to acquire the trade and assets. The main advantages of this route are: the tax history of the company (and with this any hidden tax liabilities) stays with the vendor; future tax depreciation on qualifying assets is based on purchase price not historic tax values; and the tax base cost of the assets acquired is "stepped-up" to market value (price paid). By contrast, the vendor is unlikely to want to sell assets unless only part of the business is being transferred or the vendor group has the capacity to absorb any tax charges on the assets, for example through the use of tax losses or roll-over relief capacity.

An asset sale can be particularly unattractive when the target is held by individual shareholders, as this can lead to a double charge to tax (once on the sale of the assets and then again on the extraction of the cash from the company to the shareholders).

In practice, most buy-outs will be share acquisitions. Prior to disposal, measures will often be taken by the vendor to reduce the value of the target, thereby reducing any gain on disposal. This value reduction can be achieved in a number of ways, the most common being by way of a dividend strip or a purchase of own shares. Due to recent changes in tax statute following the November 1996 budget, such planning techniques have become more complex and in particular, timing (in relation to the overall disposal) of any pre-sale dividend needs careful consideration. Any pre-sale planning undertaken by the vendor is likely to have ramifications for the purchaser and, in practice, it will be necessary to get the purchaser to agree in advance to any significant pre-sale planning techniques.

NEWCO/TARGET GROUP

Newco will be financed by a mix of debt and equity and, typically, will be highly leveraged with maximum debt and minimum equity. Debt financing is generally more attractive as interest expense (subject to certain conditions) is fully deductible for tax purposes, whereas dividends are paid out of post-tax earnings.

Dividends currently carry a 20 per cent tax credit. As a result, historically, dividends were of greater value to tax exempt institutions than interest, because the recipient could reclaim the tax credit from the Inland Revenue. However, with effect from 2 July 1997, such tax credits can no longer be reclaimed by non-tax payers.

With effect from April 1999 the tax credit will be reduced to ten per cent, even though 20 per cent of the gross dividend will be withheld on payment. For companies, the dividends received can still be used to frank an onward dividend payment; for individuals, the rate of tax applied to dividend income will be adjusted so the overall tax burden is unchanged. However, where overseas shareholders receive dividends, these changes will virtually eliminate any tax credit repayment that might otherwise have been recoverable under a tax treaty.

When determining a suitable level of debt finance, realistic profit projections will need to be reviewed to ensure all the interest expense can be tax-relieved each year. This is normally achieved through group relief, as Newco is unlikely to have a high level of taxable income itself (unless Newco acquired the trade and assets direct).

Advice on maximising the tax treatment (corporate and VAT) of these professional fees should be taken during the early stages of the transaction. Many of these expenses will be written-off to the profit and loss account, with the remaining elements being capitalised and amortised. These expenses can have a major impact on the capacity of the Newco group to absorb interest expense.

Where dividends are to be paid on shares, Newco must have sufficient distributable reserves to fund the payments, and there must be sufficient tax capacity within the Newco group to offset any ACT payable on dividends against current year corporation tax. Normally, the target company will pay the dividends to Newco with ACT so that the ACT offset is against the target's tax liability. The alternative is for dividends to be paid from target to Newco within a group income election and for Newco to pay the ACT. This will then need to be surrendered to the target for offset and, at least in the first year, this is unlikely to be possible due to the strict ACT surrender conditions. Unutilisable ACT should be avoided – it must be carried forward, and may need to be written-off against accounting profits if it cannot be recovered within one year.

One other cost that Newco will incur is stamp duty. Generally, subject to available stamp duty mitigation schemes, and the different classes of assets acquired, duty will be payable on share acquisitions at a rate of half a per cent and on asset acquisitions at a rate of one per cent on consideration of £60,000–£250,000, one and a half per cent on £250,000–£500,000 and two per cent for consideration over £500,000.

MANAGEMENT TEAM

Management will need to ensure that it obtains tax relief for any borrowings taken out to acquire shares in Newco. To ensure all the qualifying conditions are fulfilled, pre-acquisition planning needs to be undertaken. The qualifying conditions are broadly:

- *Money must be borrowed and used to acquire ordinary shares in Newco or to make a loan to Newco; an overdraft or credit card withdrawal will not qualify;*

- *Newco must be "close" at the time the investment is made (broadly controlled by five or fewer shareholders or by the company's directors); an accounting period must commence before Newco becomes non-close;*

- *From the date of investment to the date any interest is paid the individual must hold at least five per cent of the ordinary equity of Newco or work the greater part of his time managing Newco's business;*

- *When the investment is made, Newco must exist for the purpose of trading, or for holding shares in companies that trade.*

It is important to note that Newco need only be close when the investment is made and not when the interest is paid. This is achieved by ensuring that the management invests in Newco first, making it close, before the institutions inject their funds and make Newco "open". Following the case of Lord v Tustain, it is now possible for Newco to become "open" before the investment in Target is made.

The other relief that may be available to management on investment is Enterprise Initiative Scheme relief (EIS). Under the EIS there is income tax relief at 20 per cent on the first £100,000 of the investment and total exemption from capital gains on the disposal of the shares. Only new management members may qualify for the EIS relief (members who are employed by the target at the time of the buy-out are likely to be disqualified).

Employee benefit charges may apply where employees acquire shares by reason of their employment. These should not be a problem in practice, but care should be taken to ensure that the management does not acquire its shares at an undervalue, and careful planning will be needed if an equity ratchet is planned. Careful drafting of the articles of association that outline the ratchet mechanism can minimise the risk of any income gain arising.

Exit plans need to be considered at the investment stage of the buy-out, as a number of exit strategies (but by no means all) require mechanisms to be put in place from day one. Having said this, in reality exit is not the main "driver" during the structuring phase of a transaction. It is just one of many considerations.

The management team will firstly need to ensure that any gains arising will be taxed as a capital gain rather than income (see above). Having done this, various tax planning mechanisms can be applied to reduce/extinguish the gain on exit, or in some instances to defer the gain until a future capital gains disposal. These include:

■ *Pre-sale dividends;*

■ *Sale for loan note or share consideration (deferral only);*

■ *Retirement relief;*

■ *Funded Unapproved Retirement Benefit Schemes (FURBS);*

■ *Transfers to spouses, children or trust funds;*

■ *Reinvestment relief (deferral only);*

■ *EIS (part deferral);*

■ *Change of tax residency (extreme!).*

It is important that the management team starts to consider tax planning on exit well in advance of the actual exit.

VENTURE CAPITAL HOUSE

The tax position of the venture capital house will depend on the type of institution involved. In all instances, their aims will be to achieve tax-efficient extraction of funds throughout the life of the buy-out, together with a tax-efficient exit on eventual sale or flotation of Newco. The structure that will achieve this will depend on the type of institution.

Finally, the majority of recent buy-outs have centred on international transactions, raising ever more complex tax issues.

Chapter 11

Avoiding buy-out blunders

James Baird, partner, Clifford Chance, offers advice on how to avoid turning your buy-out into a catastrophe

Most members of a management buy-out team will only undergo the buy-out process once in their lives. By contrast, both the equity and debt financiers will have been involved in many such transactions and, as a result, may take for granted some of the issues which may come as a surprise to management.

APPOINTMENT OF ADVISERS

The financial backers will appoint their own advisers, including lawyers and accountants, to advise them on the transaction. In most instances the interests of these institutions and their advisers will coincide with those of management. However, in relation to management's "deal" with the equity financiers – including such items as the constitution of the company formed to carry out the buy-out, the shareholders' agreement in relation to it and in respect of service agreements – management will need its own advisers and, in particular, its own solicitor. It is important to make sure that the firm of solicitors chosen by management has experience of buy-outs, even if this means using solicitors who are unfamiliar to management, so that they can help guide the team through the issues that may arise and help it to plan ahead.

DUE DILIGENCE

The due diligence process can be painful for management unless it organises itself efficiently. The financial backers will appoint a firm of accountants to produce a voluminous report. This covers not only the financial position of the business – past, present and future – but also everything about its history and how it is run. Typically, the accountants will have spent several days at the company's premises asking management detailed questions on all manner of topics. Most often the final draft will be discussed with management before presentation to the financial backers.

Meanwhile, the financiers' solicitors will have sent a list of further questions to the vendors' solicitors. Typically, these range from corporate information, to questions about contracts, properties, employees, etc. Inevitably, the management team will be called on to collect and provide the information to answer these queries; some of the questions may cover similar ground to those questions already asked by the accountants. Other specialist advisers may then be appointed to ask yet more questions about, for example, insurance, environmental matters, property, and the company's market position.

Towards the end of the acquisition process, the vendor will be required to provide a disclosure letter to the purchaser in respect of the warranties being given by the vendor. Again, the management team will be approached by the vendors' solicitors to provide answers to the warranties, which are effectively a series of questions requiring the provision of yet more bits of paper. Many of the questions asked will cover the same ground, though from a different perspective. A well-organised management team will save time and inconvenience by distributing the workload as widely as possible. Keeping a record ready to hand of all information supplied (plus extra copies), will also save valuable time.

Finally, the management team will be asked to provide warranties to the financiers in relation to the accountants, solicitors, and other reports. The financiers will assume that the management team has been reading the various reports as matters progress. These are voluminous reports and should not be left to the last minute.

FINANCING

In addition to providing money to finance the acquisition, the financiers will be providing working capital and will replace all other existing facilities. All facilities that the business will require, including any VAT bonding arrangements, guarantees, foreign exchange hedging etc, need to be disclosed at an early stage in the transaction, as they will all have an impact on the required level of funding. Disclosing these items towards the end of the transaction will not help, since the financiers will have already fixed the appropriate levels of finance that the company can bear and it will probably not be possible to increase the amount of debt at such a late stage. The only alternative may be a price reduction, which could obviously be difficult to negotiate with the vendor at that point.

COVENANTS

Both the equity and debt financiers will place various restrictions on the way that the new company will be able to operate, including how the finances are used – how much can be spent on acquiring /disposing of assets, taking out new leases, making salary increases etc. As far as they are concerned, these will be in a fairly standard form. Do not ignore these while they are being negotiated. Once they are drawn up it will be very difficult to alter them and management will be stuck with them throughout the life of the buy-out.

If possible, ensure that the finance director attends at least some of the meetings where the loan documentation is being negotiated. It is vital that he understands how it operates so that, on completion of the buy-out, the new company can operate within its terms and not breach the covenants or the various financial ratios contained in the loan agreement. As before, it will be very difficult to re-negotiate these restrictions after they have been signed.

Indeed, immediately after the buy-out it is advisable for the board to prepare an aide memoir of the various restrictions and covenants, while the documents are still fresh in everyone's mind. This will benefit both the board and other people in the business to ensure that all such matters are complied with after the buy-out.

ADMINISTRATIVE MATTERS

The buy-out process will place considerable demands upon management resources and availability of people, particularly in the last few days when the negotiation of all the documents approaches a conclusion at the same time. It is, however, important to ensure that, in addition to the prime negotiators, other members of the management team are available and kept informed at the appropriate times. Most buy-out transactions involve the giving of financial assistance by the target and, if there are any, all of its subsidiaries. Each of the target and each subsidiary must be available to make appropriate declarations, whether or not its director is a member of the management team subscribing for shares.

Inevitably the moment for making such declarations is late at night on the day of completion. Each such director will have to attend in person – being on the end of a telephone is not good enough. As the transaction progresses, directors of such companies who are not part of the management team will need to be kept informed of when they are likely to be required to attend, and of the implications involved in making the various declarations. Similarly, board meetings of all the companies involved will probably be required, again requiring the availability of the directors.

The management team needs to ensure, therefore, that no-one is on holiday or elsewhere during the last few weeks of the buy-out. Since there may be long periods waiting around doing nothing while other bits of the buy-out transaction are negotiated and signed, suggest they bring some work with them or a good book to read!

The management team will be required to pay cash for its shares prior to the transaction being signed. It is therefore crucial that arrangements are in place for the funds to be credited into the right account at the appropriate time. Also, arrangements must be made well in advance if any management team member needs to borrow money for his investment.

CONCLUSION

Management will be placed under intense pressure, particularly throughout the later stages of the buy-out. There are many different issues that can arise and can go wrong. However, most problems are not insoluble and with planning and awareness of the types of issues that can arise, management can help to smooth the path. An appetite for late night meetings and pizzas will also help!

Chapter 12

Finding an exit route

PART ONE: THE TRADE SALE

Tim Adams, chairman of Firsteel Group, recalls the sale of his bought-out business to a large trade partner

Whenever I approach a revolving door, it reminds me of the Firsteel Group management buy-out in 1992. Just as we were negotiating the entrance, our backers, Phildrew, were asking how we intended to exit.

The group was a medium-sized engineering conglomerate, comprising three steel-processing businesses (collectively selling 150,000 tonnes of steel strip per year), and three disparate engineering companies (manufacturing process plant, road tankers and metal sections for the building industry). I could have written "desperate" as all three were losing money, their markets savaged by the recession.

Lonrho, the owner, was not prepared to sell the group piecemeal. Accordingly, the MBO and exit strategy was not the most complex to devise! Buy the group, sell the engineering companies, concentrate on the remaining steel businesses and leave their exit flexible. Phildrew positively encouraged this approach through the funding structure of the MBO. A short-term loan and expensive mezzanine finance needed to be repaid as soon as possible.

Identifying trade buyers for individual companies is relatively straightforward. It is usually the competition. The problems, of course, centre around the sensitive information required by the purchaser ahead of contract. Confidentiality agreements tend not to be worth the legal costs in drawing them up. Nevertheless, if the buyer is really interested and not merely snooping – and you must be the judge of that – the willing buyer/willing seller syndrome will prevail. We achieved our initial objective by selling the engineering companies, repaying the short-term loan on time and the mezzanine loan at its earliest redemption date in June 1994.

THREE DOWN, THE GROUP TO GO

By the Spring of 1995 we were a successful, expanding, profitable steel-processing group. We also enjoyed a close working relationship with the Strip Mill Products division of British Steel, from whom we purchased 70 per cent of our steel requirements – now running at nearly 200,000 tonnes per annum.

With our track record and current trading performance any form of exit was possible – or so we thought. The stockmarket was buoyant and yet there were few flotations in the pipeline. We were determined to have a go. Panmure Gordon was appointed as our broker and, very wisely as it turned out, suggested we put a "foot into the water" before committing ourselves. It arranged a series of short meetings with 25 potential investors. We could have lost two toes from frost bite! Forty per cent of those we met thought we were either too small – at around £32m capitalisation – or that the steel industry had peaked. On the other hand (or foot) one toe could have been bitten off. Twenty per cent could not understand why we did not go straight into the flotation, as they would be definite investors. The rest were non-committal.

Our overriding impression was of how superficial the "City" was. We were either lumped together with bulk steelmakers – despite emphasising the "speciality" of our niche products – or we were too small. We went no further. We could have floated, but Phildrew would have been left with a large percentage of the shares. The share price would have been under constant pressure and we would not have been able to raise further capital for expansion under these circumstances. There was no point in being hostage to City investors who really did not understand our business.

IT'S AN ILL WIND

Inevitably, rumours of our proposed flotation had circulated around the industry. We received a number of direct approaches along the lines of: "What are you going to do now?" The answer, and it was true, was always: "We are not under any pressure from our backers". Nevertheless we were at the crossroads. Should we borrow more, or seek further venture capital, to expand by acquisition and achieve the size required for flotation? Should we sell the less technical parts of the group, reinvest upstream and become, in the eyes of the City, specialised engineers not steelmakers, again, for a future float? Should we stay as we were and repay bankers and Phildrew from cash-flow? Or, should we explore the approaches more seriously?

By this time we were one of British Steel Strip Mill Products' biggest customers, and despite being a major competitor in some areas, we were able to discuss our dilemma with its management. In the end, despite British Steel's preference that the existing relationship should continue, it was felt that both parties' interests would be best served by British Steel acquiring the Firsteel Group (and not vice versa!!). We were about to commit the cardinal sin of trade sales, restricting ourselves to one potential purchaser.

After tortuous negotiations we finally agreed a price and entered into heads of agreement, subject to due diligence. Because we were competitors, the commercially sensitive information would only be released once all other due diligence had been completed and when both of us were confident of Office of Fair Trading (OFT) approval.

The due diligence seemed endless. All the horrors of the MBO were reincarnated. If we had been frisked by KPMG in 1992, this was an internal! If management was nervous, Phildrew had Dehli belly!

Eventually, British Steel wanted to reduce the price. After much haranguing, some falling-out and making-up, a new deal was agreed. The sensitive information was handed over, OFT approval sought and given, and our sale was concluded on the 18 April 1997.

Ours was not a text book trade sale. No competitive tendering, little involvement from the venture capitalists in the negotiations, giving away all your secrets to your biggest competitor ahead of completion. All are designed to keep your nerves on edge.

Was it a good deal? Judge for yourself. British Steel acknowledges it has purchased some very good businesses. The vast majority of Firsteel Group employees now work for a huge organisation, sympathetic to their requirements. The few people who lost their jobs were compensated generously. Phildrew earned a very good return on its investment, and I'm now off to the races!

PART TWO: FLOTATION

Dr Julian Blogh, chief executive, Ultra Electronics, recounts how his company achieved a stockmarket flotation in October 1996, following a successful MBO three years earlier

Ultra Electronics was a £39m buy-out from TI Group in October 1993. The exit route was integral to our whole MBO process from its start – and it was never far from our – or the venture capitalists' – minds. Flotation was always the likely exit route option because the specialist nature of our electronics business – a range of sub-systems for the defence and civil aerospace market – made it unlikely that a trade buyer would emerge. However, by announcing our intention to float, an opportunity was provided for trade buyers to come forward.

TIMING

About 18 months after the buy-out, we started to have initial boardroom discussions about when might be the right time to float. We took a further 18 months or so to complete the listing in 1996.

The main factor determining our timing was our ability to convince advisers that we were suitable and ready. We had to show a good record of achievement, as well as short and long-term potential. In practice, this meant explaining our investment of some £15m on expansion through acquisitions, identifying expanding markets, showing healthy forward order books and, of course, providing rigorous financial information on our past, current and projected future business performance.

About a year in advance of the float we got down to serious planning. At this stage, we had some disagreements about timing, but we were really only debating the odd six months or so. The venture capitalists were quite keen to exit quickly because stockmarket conditions were favourable and the business was in good shape. My view was that we should wait a little longer, so that we could go to the market on the back of our following year's forecast. I also felt that, as there was a general election in prospect, the likelihood was that the economy would be in reasonable shape in the second half of 1996. The downside was that an election might have been called, the stockmarket might have wobbled and we could have ended up having to delay the float. In the end, we agreed to wait.

MECHANICS OF FLOTATION

Having decided to float, we conducted a "beauty parade" to select a merchant bank to take us through the mechanics of the flotation process. The venture capitalists have experience of this process and advised us – and we duly appointed Schroders. Following the MBO, we had also appointed Peter Macfarlane as our chairman, partly because he had experience of the flotation process and had plenty of contacts in the City. He was another valuable source of advice.

Cazenove were then appointed as our brokers. We could have used an integrated merchant bank and broker, but we preferred to have two sources of advice, especially when it came to pricing the share issue. A sub-committee of the board appointed Square Mile Communications to do our financial public relations. We chose a smaller PR firm because Ultra was a fairly small company and we felt we would get more attention than from a large agency.

We had to go through a process of due diligence, carried out by Arthur Andersen which was examining the listing particulars. The process was nothing like as traumatic as the original MBO but, even so, this was a particularly frustrating document for us to produce because of the onerous conditions attached to it. Even the most self-evident statements had to be verifiable, which meant that we had to have a large team of managers gathering evidence. Of course, our company lawyers were heavily involved in the paperwork too.

The next step was to conduct a major marketing exercise, involving a string of press interviews and photographic sessions – especially with striking products, such as Eurofighter, in which some of our electronics systems are used. We were then whisked around the institutional investors in the City of London – and also Edinburgh and Glasgow – by Cazenove. In two weeks, we made more than 60 one-to-one presentations to fund managers, generating interest and potential share placings, provided the price was right.

Pricing was the final key issue to be resolved and, after thorough consultation with our advisers, a price of 250 pence per share was agreed, giving the company a market capitalisation of £162.5m. We felt the price of the placing was about right as, on the day of the flotation it reached a healthy premium at 287 pence at the close of business.

Of course, on the day of flotation we all breathed a huge sigh of relief. Ten directors shared £38m in a mixture of cash and shares. Some had had difficulties and concerns over raising the personal finance necessary to take part in the buy-out – and one or two had had to use their homes to secure finance. MBOs exert great financial and emotional pressure on the executives involved in them. Now that stage was over and we had secured our rewards. Going for a flotation can be a tough time, but not nearly so draining as the initial MBO.

AFTER THE SALE

The flotation has given the business the flexibility to raise finance through the stockmarket in the future, should we wish to – and to some extent it gives the company a higher public profile and therefore more credibility with customers. I would not overstate this advantage, however, because in our very specialised market, most potential customers know all about us anyway.

From a personal point of view, I have worked in large corporations for most of my career and I was keen on the MBO because it gave me the chance to "run my own show". I still feel we are in charge of our own affairs now, but we face different pressures. We have a much broader shareholder base, so we have to spend a lot more time talking to analysts and explaining our actions to the City. So far, this has been very enjoyable, not least because we have had a good story to tell. In 1996, we turned over nearly £124m, with pre-tax profits of more than £14m.

If I was to give advice to others contemplating a flotation as an exit route, I would say there is a clear advantage in terms of retaining freedom to run the business. With a trade sale this is less likely to be the case. But, more often than not, the choice of exit route varies according to individuals' priorities – and how best to realise value.

Chapter 13

Keeping friendly with the natives

Alan Malachowski, honorary lecturer, the universities of East Anglia and Reading, accompanies 3i plc on a trip through the jungle of MBO-speak

Good directors are like anthropologists. Before they enter new territory, they should possess at least a working-knowledge of the local language. There is probably no area of business where this facility is more important than management buy-outs.

In the complex jungle of MBOs, the 'natives' to watch out for are the so-called **intermediaries.** These engineer deals and get **the principals**, the prospective participants, round the deal table.

Intermediaries are usually agents of finance – accountants or merchant bankers. It is worth keeping them sweet, if only because of their wizardry when it comes to conjuring up profitable business opportunities. But their jargon can be baffling even to those who are otherwise fairly familiar with the venture capital industry and the arcane world of corporate finance.

As a precautionary step, a basic handbook like 3i's exemplary *Venturespeak 2000* is essential. This will prevent embarrassing elementary errors like mistaking a **Bingo** for a **Dingo**. The former signifies a buy-in-growth-opportunity with a hefty chunk of the funding designated for future growth, whereas the latter stands for: "Don't invest – no growth opportunity"!

But some sort of overall 'framework' of understanding is equally important. Simply knowing what the MBO buzzwords mean is not sufficient. It is also necessary to know when and where to use these terms, and how they hang together.

Fortunately, most MBO jargon can be slotted into four main categories for this very purpose. These are ideal for penetrating the smoke-screens that intermediaries are liable to throw up:

- *Players and markets;*

- *Types of deal;*

- *The mechanics of deals;*

- *Deal prospects.*

Be especially wary of fast-talking **vultures** – those more ruthless venture capitalists whose primary motivation is good old-fashioned greed. Expect them to resort to gobbledygook in the midst of tough negotiations, if not at the initial **beauty parade** (when potential suppliers of investment capital are put out on show – normally only on paper! – to pitch for business).

PLAYERS AND MARKETS

To keep track of buy-outs, it is essential to know the terminology for the investors and markets.

Fledgling companies need an **angel** – a successful entrepreneur who has the financial resources and street-wisdom which accrue from building up and selling a business. Other key figures are **the lead investor** who co-ordinates the activities of the relevant group of investors (or **syndicate**) and the **ringmaster** – normally an intermediary who orchestrates the whole fund raising process.

Other than the London Stock Exchange, the other rather esoteric-sounding, main markets are: **AIM** (Alternative Investment Market), **EASDAQ** (European Association of Securities Dealers Automated Quotation) and **NASDAQ** (National Association of Security Dealers Automated Quotation). Of these, the last is by far the largest, but all offer a chance to float which is easier and cheaper than a full listing.

TYPES OF DEAL

When merchant bankers allude to a **Bimbo** (not to be confused with a **Chimbo** – the investing chairman in a buy-out), they are referring to a particular kind of deal. But to understand it, we need first to be clear about a distinction within the parent category.

A management buy-out (MBO) – where the acquirers already work for the business concerned – must be sharply distinguished from a management buy-in (MBI) – where the acquirers are coming to the target business cold. Since the acquirers are self-evidently **shooting in the dark** in such cases (because they do not have inside knowledge of the business), MBIs clearly carry a higher prima facie risk. By the same token, the backers will need that much more convincing they have a **sleeping beauty** on their hands – a business of great, but as-yet-unawakened, potential. Sharp and useful though this distinction is, canny deal-makers have found a way to cut across it. A **Bimbo** is a buy-in-management-buy-out: a combination of an MBI and an MBO, where an entrepreneurial manager moves in on a company and then forms an alliance with in-house managers to run it independently.

Other terms for deals tend to wear their meaning on their sleeves. In an **institutional buy-out** (IBO), sometimes called a **financial purchase**, a financial institution acquires a business and then installs its own choice of managers. **Leveraged buy-outs** (LBOs) involve high levels of debt, or **gearing** (the ratio of debt to equity capital). When employees are in on the deal alongside management, this is called a management and employee buy-out (**Mebo**). Finally, an **owner buy-out** is exactly what it appears to be, as is a **secondary buy-out** or **buy-out of a buy-out**, where the original MBO managers sell on to a further generation of managers.

THE MECHANICS OF DEALS

It is one thing to know what different kinds of buy-out are called, but what about their 'mechanics' – their internal workings, processing and structure?

Forget de-layering or downsizing – which are just euphemisms for cutting staff – it is here that details of funding matter most and the financial lingo of the intermediaries kicks in. They may size up a deal according to **discounted cash-flow**, where the value of an investment is assessed by predicting future cash-flows which have been 'discounted' to take into account the value of money over time.

A deal could include a **deferred consideration** – which means an element of the transaction is to be paid at a later stage, and perhaps tied to performance targets. **Dividend cover** could also be a hot topic. This is the ratio dictating the number of times a dividend could have been paid out of a year's earnings. The higher the cover, the 'safer' the investment. When relatively small companies are involved, **growth** or **development capital** is likely to be a talking point. **Equity capital** of this kind is raised to fund ambitious long-term growth without too much bank debt – the small, private company's equivalent of rights issues on the stockmarket. And, in all buy-outs, everyone keeps a keen eye on the level of **directors' emoluments** which include costly benefits such as special expenses and pension arrangements.

DEAL PROSPECTS

MBO-speak comes into its own when describing how good a deal looks, how it is going and how it is likely to turn out in the end.

Terms of approbation are obvious. The eyes of intermediaries glisten at the mention of a **pearl** or **gem**. But they look closely for **the downside**, eke out **the worst case scenarios** and analyse the **comfort factors** (features of the business, such as branding and customer relations, which put a good complexion on the risks). They do this to avoid a **dog** – bad investment – or a **Bambi** – a bloody awful MBI. They will also keep **the exit** in the back of their minds at all times. This is the opportunity for investors to **realise** (sell) their investment. In the meantime, if unfortunately things do go wrong, a **Rambo** may be required – a rescue after an MBO.

CODA

Intermediaries are quick on their feet, and sometimes the only way to keep up with them is to improvise. You have to be prepared to make things up as you go along, as I did on two occasions above: **shooting in the dark** and **sleeping beauty** are not really part of the MBO lexicon. At least not yet!

AN MBO TIMETABLE

It is possible to complete an MBO within a six week timescale from initial identification of the opportunity to completion. However, this will only be achieved where all parties are keen to progress the transaction rapidly, information required is available and flows freely and the business to be acquired is relatively discreet and operates from a small number of locations. More typically, buy-outs will take between three and six months.

An MBO involves the following main steps:

- *Identify opportunity and write business plan;*
- *Management: organise, select adviser, finalise business plan;*
- *Appoint deal leader;*
- *Identify sources of finance;*
- *Agree outline terms with vendor;*
- *Conduct due diligence;*
- *Negotiate legal documentation;*
- *Completion.*

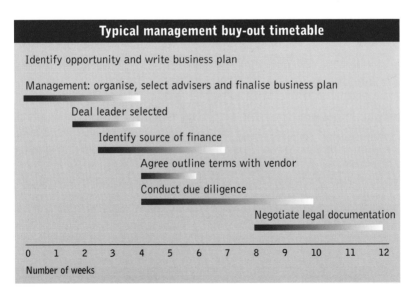

Typical management buy-out timetable

Identify opportunity and write business plan

Management: organise, select advisers and finalise business plan

Deal leader selected

Identify source of finance

Agree outline terms with vendor

Conduct due diligence

Negotiate legal documentation

0 1 2 3 4 5 6 7 8 9 10 11 12

Number of weeks

AN MBO CHECKLIST

Is there a deal?

■ *Will the parent company sell to the management team?*

■ *Will the company be better of as an independent company?*

■ *Is the current management team up to the task?*

■ *Are the cash-flows sufficiently positive and predictable that finance can be raised to buy the business?*

■ *Can you all make money on this and can you agree the "exit"?*

■ *Will your domestic life take the strain of carrying out an MBO?*

The initial steps

■ *Do you have the support of your colleagues?*

■ *Approach the parent company for permission to prepare an offer;*

■ *Assuming permission granted, prepare a three to five-year business plan for the business;*

■ *Decide whether or not you need a financial adviser;*

■ *If so, appoint and agree his terms of reference and his fees;*

■ *Financial adviser to confirm a deal is possible;*

■ *Approach venture capital houses and appoint a lead investor;*

■ *Do not forget to keep running the business.*

The nitty gritty

■ *Detailed offer to parent company;*

■ *Finalise financial structure and partners, including choice of bank;*

■ *Sort out personal financial issues and tax planning;*

■ *Agree a sensible timetable and try to keep to it;*

■ *Detailed due diligence commences – do not forget that financiers will need access to company and customers, and lots of your time to ask damn-fool questions;*

- *Independent accountants' review – yet more silly questions and time taken up;*
- *Pensions – have they been forgotten about again?*
- *Properties – if there are many of them, ensure your files are in good shape at the outset; Do not forget to keep running the business.*

The legal stages

- *Sale and purchase agreement;*
- *Articles and shareholders agreement for "Newco";*
- *Service agreements;*
- *Banking documentation;*
- *Review the timetable;*
- *Avoid unnecessary meetings and get everyone to mark up their comments clearly on documents;*
- *Again, do not forget to keep running the business.*

Completion

- *Are you absolutely sure you still want to carry on?*
- *Are you absolutely sure the business is adequately funded as statutory declarations to that effect are likely to be required?*
- *Have you disclosed everything to your financial partners especially recent weeks' performance – or has it slipped because you have forgotten something?*
- *Bring a sleeping bag.*

Post completion

- *Get back down to earth and keep your eye firmly on that exit;*
- *Save the real celebration till then;*
- *The true heroes are those who survive the course.*